Praise from Lorraine Murphy's mentees

'Working with Lorraine has been an opportunity to take stock of all aspects of my life. To be guided by Lorraine's wisdom and straightforward approach to getting shit done means that I have been able to put simple strategies in place to get more done with less stress. Lorraine's goal-setting guidance has been invaluable to me. As someone who needs external accountability, Lorraine has provided that and so much more. She is like an accountability angel who walks the walk and talks the talk! Lorraine is brave, big-hearted and oh so wise!' – **Bernadette**

'Lorraine has allowed me to step into myself by proving to me that all I need is to believe in myself. She has taught me to trust my instincts, vouch for myself, ask for what I want and look after myself. By doing her courses, both online and in real life, reading her books and being a part of her membership group, she's shown me how to manage my own energy and mindset while successfully navigating three kids, a husband, a dog, a household and almost full-time work – but importantly still taking time to look after myself. I'm forever indebted to her for her confidence in me and her tough love.' – **Kylie**

'In life, there's goal setters and then there's goal getters. Of all the things Lorraine has taught me, it's been how to move from the former to the latter. What once were pipedreams (aka crumpled pieces of paper left to perish in a drawer somewhere) are now goals that have been actioned. From helping me set more realistic goals in the first

place, to breaking them into bite-sized chunks and, most importantly, implementing them immediately to create behavioural change, I have been able to achieve what I want to in business and in my personal life thanks to Lorraine's advice.' – **Hannah**

'Working with Lorraine was absolutely pivotal in my journey to make a HUGE career change and pursue my lifelong passion! This ultimately led me to a place of immense happiness and I feel like I'm finally where I am meant to be in my life! Lorraine was my coach, cheerleader, sounding board and advisor during our mentoring program. She gave me guidance and mindset tools to overcome roadblocks and hurdles that had been there for YEARS. I did the "hard work" but without Lorraine's guidance, I couldn't have made the changes I made.' – **Alexis**

'I first attended Lorraine's Get Remarkably Organised workshop in Melbourne in 2018. Since then, Lorraine has become one of my most important mentors, enabling me to do more, to be a better person and therefore support my clients in a more meaningful way. While I have loved all of Lorraine's programs, books and group mentoring, it's the one-on-one coaching that has enabled the most meaningful change. My live mentoring with her on her podcast in 2020 enabled real understanding of the importance of energy management and gave me steps to implement that have stuck. Relistening to it a year later reinforced how much I needed that support and how much her mentoring helped me to manage the overwhelm I was feeling at the time.' – **Sarah**

'Lorraine has helped me step into myself by teaching me the importance of positive self-talk, energy management, goal setting and staying on track. Since completing many of her online programs, reading her books and being a part of her membership group, I have grown and learnt so much about myself, what I want and what I am capable of. She is a brilliant sounding board and will never tell you what you want to hear, but what you need to hear. Lorraine is also an expert at breaking down all the steps for you, so you don't feel overwhelmed and you can achieve what you are striving for – whether it be personal or business related, she's got you covered. I am so grateful to have her wisdom and guidance in my life.' – **Caitlin**

'Something I have always struggled with is my energy management. Lorraine identified that booking in a half day of tank-filling time or a learning day once a month would be beneficial to my energy. Even just having this in my schedule has been a game changer, so I can't wait to see the results. The only way I can really describe Lorraine's impact is that I am living more true to myself than I have before. Lorraine triggered a spiritual exploration that I will always be grateful for.' – **Liz**

STEP INTO You

ALSO BY LORRAINE MURPHY

Remarkability
Get Remarkably Organised
Baby, You're Remarkable

How to
Rediscover Your
Extraordinary Self

STEP
INTO
You

LORRAINE
MURPHY

hachette
AUSTRALIA

IMPORTANT NOTE TO READERS: Although every effort has been made to ensure that the contents of this book are accurate, it must not be treated as a substitute for qualified medical advice. Always consult a qualified medical practitioner. Neither the author nor the publisher can be held responsible for any loss or claim arising out of the use, or misuse, of the suggestions made or the failure to take advice.

hachette
AUSTRALIA

Published in Australia and New Zealand in 2022
by Hachette Australia
(an imprint of Hachette Australia Pty Limited)
Gadigal Country, Level 17, 207 Kent Street, Sydney, NSW 2000
www.hachette.com.au

Hachette Australia acknowledges and pays our respects to the past, present and future Traditional Owners and Custodians of Country throughout Australia and recognises the continuation of cultural, spiritual and educational practices of Aboriginal and Torres Strait Islander peoples. Our head office is located on the lands of the Gadigal people of the Eora Nation.

NATIONAL
LIBRARY
OF AUSTRALIA

A catalogue record for this book is available from the National Library of Australia

ISBN: 978 0 7336 4768 0 (paperback)

Cover design by Christabella Designs
Cover design inspiration from Lily Partridge
Author photograph courtesy of Gregory Eckels
Typeset in 12/18.7 pt Adobe Caslon Pro by Bookhouse, Sydney
Printed and bound in Australia by McPherson's Printing Group

MIX
Paper from
responsible sources
FSC
www.fsc.org   FSC® C001695

The paper this book is printed on is certified against the Forest Stewardship Council® Standards. McPherson's Printing Group holds FSC® chain of custody certification SA-COC-005379. FSC® promotes environmentally responsible, socially beneficial and economically viable management of the world's forests.

Dedicated to every woman who has opened her life to me:
this book is by you and for you.

CONTENTS

Part 5 THE HOTSPOTS

ABOUT THIS BOOK

I'm thrilled you've joined me for this Step Into You journey – a journey into YOU and the life you wish to live.

This book has been shaped from the learnings of many years of me leading one-on-one mentoring, retreats, workshops and live support sessions. It's also come from my own experiences: the crushing pain of losses, failures and disappointments, and the elation of the wins, connections and progress.

Everything I'm about to share with you in this book has come from hard-won lessons. I'm passionate about passing them on to other women so that they can benefit from them.

I've had the privilege of accessing the innermost thoughts of thousands of women through my work – women just like you. Women who want to find more direction, feel more motivated, manage their time better, have stronger self-awareness . . . and who seek to be empowered with a tailored plan to live a more fulfilling version of their lives.

If that's what you're after, my dear, you've come to the right place!

Over these pages, I'll pass on the core principles, as well as valuable 'I never knew that' tips, advice and hacks that have transformed my life and the lives of my mentees. Then I'll bring the theory to life with real, raw and relatable examples from my own life, my retreat attendees and my online program participants.

I want you to feel, as you move through this book, that you're having a juicy, nugget-laden chat with a trusted BFF over a leisurely ladies' lunch. (I'm putting in a special request for my favourites: salt-and-pepper calamari, fries and prosecco – please, and thanks!)

I know that many women – maybe you included – are overwhelmed, lacking purpose, feeling lost and out of touch with themselves. I call it being a 'low res' version of themselves. They're lacking the confidence, the motivation and the framework for their own personal version of success, and they're also likely to be lacking the support needed to help them make positive changes in their lives.

They've prioritised careers, families, partners and communities over themselves – at the expense of their own success, health and wellbeing. Women deserve better than this. *You* deserve better than this!

We need women to be the brightest expression of themselves in order to create a world we can all be proud of. There is a societal, cultural and economic Zeitgeist of women's empowerment – the divine feminine is most definitely on the rise, and thank God for that. However, the gap between where women are right now and where they want to be is vast.

It's an ambitious vision, but I believe this book can help women bridge that gap. By stepping into our fullest potential as women, we can be the change we wish to see in the world.

This doesn't just happen. It requires a deep dive into self-awareness. It requires the knowledge and tools to make the shifts we wish to make. It requires the support of people we trust. *It requires an infrastructure.*

My intent in writing this book is to create an infrastructure that will help you step into the lightest and brightest representation of you possible. By picking up this book, you're saying that you're now ready to step into that version of yourself.

IMPORTANT NOTE

This book is NOT about putting pressure on yourself to perform/create/deliver/kill it/smash it/knock it out of the park.

I've got a pretty good idea that you're already quite adept at putting pressure on yourself, and the last thing you need is me yelling in your face – especially if you're feeling in a less-than-optimum frame of mind right now.

Having a mentor is not an option for everyone, budget- or time-wise. I'm hoping that owning this book will be like having a mentor in your pocket – one that you can consult at any time and at a pace that suits your growth journey.

A LITTLE ABOUT ME AND MY APPROACH

So here I am offering myself as your mentor – and I haven't even introduced myself!

I became an entrepreneur in 2012 and after selling my first company, a social media business, in 2017, I've since focused on my 'soul-on-fire' work: writing, speaking and mentoring.

My purpose? To help women rise even higher in their lives by sharing with them new skills to embrace the power of self-prioritisation and self-knowledge. (You and I will be talking a lot more about purpose in Chapter 6!)

My current business offers online programs, one-on-one mentoring, events (virtual and IRL), retreats, and of course books like this one. This is my fourth book, and I am quite literally giddy with excitement that I get to share it with you.

I'm originally from Dublin, Ireland, and arrived in Sydney, Australia, in February 2009 via a three-year working stint in London. I landed with my British boyfriend of the time, with the vague plan of spending a year somewhere infinitely more sunny than London – and have been here ever since.

My relationship broke up within three months, and I set myself the lofty goal of being single for 18 months and meeting my future husband at that point. Within five months, on a random doorstep, I happened across the force of nature and beam of light that is my husband, Wade. We were married on that same doorstep three years later.

A few months before our wedding I'd started my first business, and with it came the greatest personal development exercise of my life. After six months of solid pushing shit uphill, the business began to gain momentum and went on to be a success. Myself and my team won a shelf-full of awards, generated annual revenue in the multi-millions and I got to have life-changing experiences, like spending a week on Necker Island with Sir Richard Branson.

The day before I flew to Necker Island in 2016, my first book, *Remarkability*, was published. It featured my tales from the frontline of starting a business.

After keeping us waiting for a while, our daughter Lexi arrived in June 2017 – and has filled our lives with pure joy and magic ever since . . . along with a solid dose of challenge!

I wrote my second book, *Get Remarkably Organised*, while very pregnant with Lexi and then with her sleeping next to me as a tiny newborn. That book has been described by many readers as their 'bible' on all things organisation. My third book told the story of building a business alongside building a family – that one's called *Baby, You're Remarkable*. And just as I finished the first draft of this book, our baby boy Wilder joined us.

Now, I want to share a particular story with you . . .

A couple of years ago, I put myself into therapy. I had recently read Dolly Alderton's memoir *Everything I Know About Love*, and her story of going through therapy normalised it as something that 'regular' people did.

I know, it sounds crazy, doesn't it? All the coaching/alternative therapies/seminars/personal development I'd pursued over the years, and therapy somehow seemed like something a bit too 'out there'!

In the first session, my psychologist, Fiona, asked me a ton of questions about what had brought me to her sofa. And I talked . . . and cried . . . and talked some more. There was business stuff, family stuff, relationship stuff, health stuff – I dumped it all.

Once I'd finished, she looked at me very calmly and said, *'Lorraine, you need a soft place to land.'* And I promptly burst into tears again, because she was SO RIGHT! Her words touched a place deep in my soul, a place that knew her words were absolute truth for me. Home felt hard, relationships felt hard, work felt hard. To be very honest with you, the only part of my life that didn't feel hard was Lexi.

Fiona's sofa became my soft place to land during that tough time, and – gradually – the other areas of my life started to soften too. Things began to fall into place in my business, and my confidence grew, relationships started to heal, and I felt a lot more secure in my life. I built softness into my days and started to feel more like 'me' than I had in a long time.

Six months after that first conversation with Fiona, I decided that I wanted to create my own soft place to land for those who needed it in my community . . . and my Step Into You philosophy was born. Step Into You started life as an online program in 2019 and has run three times since then. Participants have described it in these ways:

'A great program for anyone who wants to increase their energy and return or move closer to their dream life, without a drill-sergeant style coach who is going to make them feel bad or guilty for not moving fast enough.'

'A gentle way to find clarity . . . without feeling completely overwhelmed.'

'A swift kick up the butt whilst simultaneously offering a warm hug – the perfect balance!'

Based on feedback of hundreds of participants to date, it was clear to me that a book was needed that would expand on the concepts I shared in the program. Happily, my wonderful publisher Hachette Australia agreed, and here you and I are today!

HOW TO READ THIS BOOK

The best way to read this book is to move through it in the order I've created it. Each section is designed to flow on and build from the previous section – exactly how I'd structure a one-on-one mentoring program with you. *However,* if you're in need of SOS support in a specific area, feel free to jump right into the chapter you feel will help you – then come back and start reading from the beginning when you're ready.

RESOURCES

Before you turn to the following chapters, please download your Step Into You Playbook for free from my website at lorrainemurphy. com.au/playbook. This playbook is a bumper pack of worksheets and tools that I'll refer to at relevant points throughout the book. Keep it handy so you can deep-dive into your Step Into You journey, engage with the activities and reap the full benefits. Then at the end of the book you'll find a list of recommended reading to help you explore some of the concepts I'll introduce you to further.

Now, grab a blanket and stuff a cushion behind your back. We're getting started . . .

Part 1

Prepare your mindset

My intention for this opening section is to help you release certain toxic ways of thinking so you can move forward in your Step Into You journey free of any mindset limitations.

Chapter 1

TRUTH BOMBS

OKAY, MY DEAR, THIS IS THE START OF OUR STEP INTO YOU JOURNEY.

One of the first things I do at the beginning of a new year, or whenever there's a new chapter about to unfold (a house move, pregnancy, a new business venture), is to do a thorough declutter of the house.

The reason? Clearing the decks of physical clutter also helps to clear the mental clutter. And the mental bandwidth that this frees up sets me up for maximum success – whether that's with making my annual goals a reality, or with a new business project.

The purpose of this chapter is to clear you of a very specific kind of mental clutter: the toxic mindset blocks that hold you back. From my work with thousands of women, I've found that these blocks are the most common. They hold women back, keep them playing small and lead to varying degrees of pain and frustration.

In this chapter I'll share with you the seven most common mindset limitations I have identified – and unleash the truth bombs that will help you overcome them.

Let's get stuck in . . .

1. SOMETHING IS WRONG WITH ME

There is *big* business in making women feel like there's something wrong with them – from the cosmetics industry to personal development, convincing us that we're in some way lacking generates billions of dollars in profit for companies.

From my work with thousands of women, I have realised that we very often view challenges in our lives as a reflection on us, as if we have fallen short in some way. We then convince ourselves that we are freakish/strange in having that challenge, and we feel too ashamed or embarrassed to talk about it with the people around us. But I'm yet to come across a challenge that's unique to one woman alone.

Research professor Brené Brown states in her book *Daring Greatly* that silence is an essential ingredient in maintaining shame. The less we talk about a concern, the more ashamed we feel, and this makes us even less inclined to talk about it. And so the shame cycle is created.

I've experienced this myself.

For years I thought I was 'abnormal' when it came to sex. I convinced myself that everyone around me was having waaay more sex than I was. My lower-than-'average' (whatever that is!) sex drive was something that weighed on my heart for far too long, and caused not insignificant tension in my marriage.

4

Last year I got so sick of that heaviness that I decided to take some proactive steps on 'fixing' myself. (But I didn't understand at that point that there was nothing wrong with me!)

As I started to unpick my sexual anxieties, I gingerly began talking to close friends about sex. For the most part it was the first time we'd ever spoken about it together, and I cannot tell you the relief they felt to have the subject broached! Through those conversations, I very quickly realised that each of us had our own worries and hang-ups when it came to this sensitive area.

Fast forward a few months . . .

Based on the revelations I had about sex last year, I created a podcast episode purely on that topic. I was *terrified* of putting myself out there so openly. However, I figured that even if just one woman was helped by my disclosures, it would have been worth it.

I had no idea how big an impact the episode would have. In just one week it became the most popular episode of my podcast since I'd begun the show 18 months earlier. I had hundreds of messages from women thanking me for helping them to feel 'normal' (again, whatever that is).

MY TRUTH BOMB *for you*

The most painful things in our lives are the most difficult to talk about, even (especially!) with our close friends and family. Whatever your challenge right now – sex, work, money, family, health – you are not alone. And I'll issue you with a rock-solid guarantee: your problem is not unique.

2. I'M NOT WORTHY OF BETTER

I believe that the very first trip-wire to us getting stuck in lives that are not lighting us up is the belief that we're not worthy of any better.

Average marriage? *I'm not worthy of a wonderful relationship.*

Persistent financial difficulties? *I don't deserve the money I dream of.*

Dissatisfaction with health? *I deserve the lack of fitness/extra weight/low energy.*

A few months ago, I hosted a retreat run by my fellow mentor Michelle Broadbent for a group of established entrepreneurs. Michelle was running one particular session, which was geared at helping the women design their ideal support team for their businesses. I was curled up in an armchair, enjoying getting to be an observer for a change.

Two of the group had experienced ongoing issues with getting the 'right' person to manage the admin side of their businesses – I'm talking for years, here. As Michelle got into the do's and don'ts of securing a support team 'unicorn' (what we call a total rockstar hire!), both of these women raised the issues that they'd had in the past.

I came to a sudden realisation as I listened to the conversation from my cosy chair: the problem wasn't *how* they were trying to recruit these team members, it was *what* they believed they deserved.

I butted in (sorry, Michelle!) and said: *'Here's the thing, ladies. Finding great team members is like finding the partner of our dreams. If we believe we're only worthy of average treatment, then we're going to find a partner who treats us as average. If we believe we're worthy of great respect, love and kindness, then we'll find a partner who can provide us with that.*

'I don't think the problem is that you're going the wrong way about hiring these people. The problem is that you believe you're only worthy of substandard support in your business. And it's not true! Get yourselves believing that you're worthy of excellent support, and you'll find it.'

A month later, one of the women, Liz, had hired an assistant, who could support her in her business. Apparently she came with serious unicorn credentials!

MY TRUTH BOMB *for you*

You are NOT an average person and you DO NOT deserve an average life. You are brilliant, clever, talented and resourceful. And you sure as fuck are worthy of anything you dream of in your life.

3. PEOPLE DON'T APPROVE

A few months ago I hosted a virtual training session for a group of university students who were in the process of starting side hustles. At the very outset of the session I explained that our hour together wasn't going to be about me listing my achievements and how I got there, but about me helping them through their biggest obstacles when it came to starting their fledgling businesses.

Rapidly, they each shared their obstacles.

One said: *'People saying "I told you so" when you fail.'*

Another said: *'Family and friends telling you that you can't/won't succeed.'*

And another said: *'Judgement from other people, like friends and family.'*

Stepping out in a different direction from the one familiar to those who've known us for most or all of our lives can be absolutely terrifying. From when we were tiny kids, we have sought the approval and affirmation of our parents, caregivers and siblings – and later on, our friends.

Doing something new, and something that those close to us may not have done before, is daunting to say the least.

When I went to a three-day event run by motivational speaker Tony Robbins, Tony asked the thousands of people assembled to raise their hands if someone in their lives was concerned about them being at the event. To my surprise, at least a quarter of the audience raised their hands.

Tony explained that the people who care about us simply want to keep us safe. When they see us doing something new – like starting a business, taking up a new hobby, committing to a financial investment, even falling in love – they can get worried. *'What if it doesn't work and they get hurt?'* they think. And often, out of pure love, they might try to dissuade us from taking that next step in whatever our venture is.

It can be soul-destroying when a parent or trusted 'grown-up' in our lives doesn't approve of our life choices – and it can certainly put a major dampener on Christmas and other family events!

This is particularly difficult when that person has no experience of what you're doing.

A couple of years ago I hosted a group from my community for dinner in Brisbane. One of my guests, a dance teacher, shared an online business idea she had within the dance industry. It was super-smart and solved an obvious problem . . . so I immediately got excited for her.

'I probably won't ever do it though,' she said sadly, gazing down at her plate. *'But why?'* I asked, *'it's a brilliant idea!'* She explained that she had shared the idea with her childhood dance teacher, who had not seen the value in it – and had very clearly shared that opinion with her. This conversation had happened two years beforehand, and she had stopped working on the idea all that time ago.

I need to note here that this past dance teacher was in her seventies and had little to no experience of online businesses. But my dinner guest respected her opinion so much – even on a topic she had no authority on! – that she parked her kick-ass business idea.

MY TRUTH BOMB *for you*

Remember that the people who love us want to keep us safe, and if that means us not changing, then often that can be A-okay with them. It's for you to keep your eye on your own aspirations, and to navigate that love/fear combo as gracefully and courageously as you can.

4. I'M NOT SIGNIFICANT

So many women gave so much before us to allow us to have the opportunities we have today. They fought for us to vote, to make money, to choose whether or not to have children, to travel, to start businesses. And, sadly, in many parts of the world they're still fighting.

Millions and millions more women sacrificed their lives for the lives of others – mostly for their husbands and children. And – as I see in my community every day – they're still sacrificing.

We are the most liberated generation of women that has existed in recent history. Therefore we owe it to those women who paved the way for us to live the biggest, brightest lives we can.

And we must also keep in our sight all the females looking to us to be an example of what it means to be a woman. Our children, for sure, but there are other women who have encountered you – at a store, in a group gathering, in a passing conversation – whose internal blueprint of what a woman is has been partly defined by you.

This could be seen as an onerous responsibility, but I choose to see it as a tremendous opportunity. What kind of woman do you want to be? Kind, brave, vulnerable, generous, outspoken, passionate, calm? A cocktail of all of the above? Be that woman for you, for the women who preceded you and for the women watching you today.

It can be incredibly difficult for a woman to make the decision to improve her life purely for her own benefit – particularly if she's been putting everyone and everything further up her priority list than herself for years. But when I (gently) ask her what sort of person she is modelling for the children in her life, she quickly recognises the broader influence her unhappiness or 'stuckness' is having.

Most of my girlfriends and the women in my community acknowledge that their mothers modelled the 'martyr' for them as they grew up – me included. Our mothers went without, had little or no time for themselves and generally put themselves bottom of the pecking order in the context of family life. And it makes sense: that's what they saw their mothers do, and their mothers before that.

I find myself slipping into martyr mode often – and it's taken tremendous work on myself to a) become aware of when I'm doing it, and b) create a new pattern. This has at times felt like turning the *Titanic*, so entrenched in my DNA is the *'a good woman is selfless'* story.

I passionately do not want our daughter to grow up emulating this pattern – and that gives me the fuel to turn that *Titanic* around, even when it feels hopeless or exhausting.

MY TRUTH BOMB *for you*

You have ENORMOUS significance: your life is a testament to all the women who went before you, and to all the women looking to you right now, today, as a model for who and what a woman can be.

5. I NEED TO CHANGE OTHER PEOPLE BEFORE I CAN BE HAPPY

Okay, I am still learning to change this unproductive mindset! I've expended enormous energy on trying to change other people – especially my husband. I desperately want him to be more like me, as I believe I am right. All. Of. The. Time.

We had a great family Sunday a few months before Wilder was born. We drove to one of our favourite walks: through a mangrove, a short bush track uphill, a cruisy walk down, arriving by the water for a paddle at a pebble beach. We got home three hours later, the three of us pretty wiped out after all the activity. We unloaded the car, and I inwardly sighed as I listed the things I had to do: get Lexi bathed, sort out her bag from her sleepover the night before, pack the groceries away, clear one more load of laundry, tee up dinner . . . Honestly, all I wanted to do was hit the sofa and veg out, but I powered on.

Five minutes after we arrived home, Wade announced he was going upstairs for a nap. *A nap!! With so much to do?!* I listed everything that needed to be done, clearly requesting he join me in tackling that list. He made me agree not to do it just yet (I totally lied) and off he went. I hit the groceries hard and got Lexi into the bath, all the while resenting the fact that he was resting upstairs. Then the shit hit the fan – I won't bore you with the details but, in summary, we had a Mexican stand-off about washing her hair. She yelled, I yelled . . . and when Wade came stumbling down the stairs into WWIII, he proceeded to lecture me on how I was just making everyone's life harder.

I was FUMING! In my mind, I was taking one for the team by pushing through all the tasks that needed to be done. *I was a hero!* And as my reward, I was being hit by revolt (her) and criticism (him).

I kicked the two of them out of the bathroom, had a shower and took myself up to our bedroom to read my book. I fell asleep, then woke up to find Wade sweeping the front garden path. I realised then that the previous hour would have looked totally different if I had chosen to accept his opinion, and allow myself to rest FIRST.

At that moment, my core belief was: *'I cannot rest when there is work to do.'*

Wade's core belief was: *'I will rest when I need to, and get the work done later.'*

Both of us were firmly convinced that our core belief was the 'right' one – and nothing either of us said would have convinced the other otherwise.

MY TRUTH BOMB *for you*

Let's agree at the outset of this book that YOU are the focus for any changes, and that your efforts throughout this book will be centred on yourself and not changing the people around you. The most effective overall transformation comes from us changing. And guess what? When we change, those around us start to change too! (But that's not why we do it, of course.)

6. I'M NOT AS GOOD AS OTHERS

If there is one thing that's guaranteed to kill our mindset and motivation, it's comparing our lives to the lives of others.

I'm sure I'm not alone in mentally score-carding myself on my outfit/make-up/hair/crow's-feet when I'm out at an event. In lightning-quick time I evaluate all the other women there and as a result I feel either a) great, as I decide I measure up well against them, or b) shit, as they're all fitter/better-dressed/younger-looking/ have bouncier hair than me.

This 'comparisonitis' (as author and podcast host Melissa Ambrosini calls it in her book of the same name) is instilled in us from very early on - particularly when it comes to our appearance. Observing how adults interact with our daughter, it is incredible how many people will comment on her hair, her eyes or her clothes. Whereas her little boy friends seem to be spared that kind of appraisal.

But the comparisonitis doesn't stop with how we look.

We look around our gym class and benchmark the strength and fitness of our bodies against that of other women, or how our children are dressed compared to other people's kids, or how many books we read last year compared to our colleague . . . On and on the comparisonitis goes.

Then we have social media to thank for making it endlessly possible to compare ourselves to people online – the vast majority of whom are total strangers who we will never meet, and whose true lives are unknown to us.

Here's what I've learned: comparing myself to someone else is a no-win game. If I feel I've come out on top of the comparison, I feel superior, 'judgey' and snooty. If I come out on the bottom of the comparison, I feel like crap about myself on that point of comparison . . . and everything else in my life, while I'm at it.

I've also learned that when I discover the full story behind the tiny snippet we get to see of others' lives, the reality is often not as perfect as I thought. That perfect couple with their perfect life? They'd been enduring a private struggle to conceive a baby. The friends building the dream 'forever home'? Heavy financial stress in order to cover the cost of the build. Time and time again I've been shown that my comparisonitis is not accurate – and it's definitely not serving me any benefits.

MY TRUTH BOMB *for you*

Holding yourself up against other people will result in you taking one step forward in your own growth and then immediately taking two steps back – and that's not for you, my dear. Become aware of all the ways you compare yourself to others, and give yourself permission to let it go. All of it.

7. I'M STUCK IN THIS SITUATION

One of my friends, Rachel MacDonald, is a business coach and a very wise woman. She likes to talk about the idea that, just like in nature, life moves in seasons. It's an idea I've grown to love.

Sometimes we can feel totally and utterly stuck. You convince yourself that things will never get better/easier/more restful.

Here's an example. You become a mother for the first time, and those newborn days (and nights!) feel endless. Days blend into each other, with a succession of nappies, vomit mop-ups and feeds. And then, one day, things start to feel a tiny bit easier. And a few days later, easier still. Until, probably without you even noticing it, you've emerged from that season into the next season.

I've had many seasons in my life:

- selling my first business and starting my second: a season of grief for what was, and nervous excitement for what lay ahead
- meeting and falling in love with Wade: a season of being on Cloud Nine
- recovering from the trauma of two miscarriages within two months: a season of believing my heart would always feel totally broken

They were JUST SEASONS!

It's so important to acknowledge the particular mood, state or position we're in – and know that it's not a permanent situation. Time will organically move us out of that season (e.g. children will grow older), or we can take proactive steps to start to move beyond that season (e.g. to quit a role we're not loving and take on a new one).

MY TRUTH BOMB *for you*

Do not tell yourself the bullshit story that you are stranded in your particular season, with no rescue boat on the horizon. You are your own rescue boat.

Acknowledge where you're at right now. Acknowledge where you'd like to be. And create three steps that will get you on your way. That's your rescue boat right there.

And if you're in a happy season, soak that shit up! Enjoy the fulfilment and success coming your way. Life is life, and more seasons will follow.

Please remember: ﹌﹌﹌﹌﹌﹌﹌

Before we wrap up this chapter together, let's recap the mindset patterns we've talked about.

- Nothing is wrong with you. And your problems are not unique.
- You are worthy of anything you dream of in your life.
- If friends and family hold you back, know that it's likely only out of love and concern for you, and remember it's your responsibility to navigate your own dreams.
- You are a significant model of what a woman can be, both for the women who went before you, and the ones who are looking to you right now.
- The only person you can change is you.
- Comparing yourself to others is a no-win game.
- Embrace the season you're in right now.

I'm so proud of you for being open to considering how these toxic mindset blocks play out in your life. When we become aware of such blocks, we can do something about them. We bring them from the dark into the light, and there we can begin to heal and shift them. To paraphrase American poet Maya Angelou's famous words, when we know better, we can do better.

Part 2

Start with your energy

In the following chapters I will share with you how to take stock of where your life is at right now and how to generate more energy day to day – and sustain it.

Chapter 2

GET OUT OF OVERWHELM

ONE OF THE BIGGEST CHALLENGES THAT I SEE WOMEN FACING IS a lack of energy. They get stuck in a rut, they begin to feel overwhelmed, the overwhelm lowers their energy, it becomes impossible to dig themselves out of the rut, and so the cycle continues.

Overwhelm results in this feeling of 'stuckness', low motivation and lack of enthusiasm for life generally. And if we don't haul our asses out of that rut, we spiral down into inertia, exhaustion, and maybe anxiety and depression.

Believe me, I've been there: bought the T-shirt, worn that T-shirt out and bought another one . . . in multiple colourways.

I've figured out a number of strategies to boost my energy, and I've shared these with my mentees over the years. These are long-term approaches that build and sustain energy over a long period of time. We'll jump into them in the next chapter but right now we're starting with getting you a fast-track pass out of Overwhelm Hell.

WHY ARE WOMEN SO EXHAUSTED?

Let's start with an exhaustive (ha!) list of what has so many of us feeling like a teabag that's been dunked too many times.

1. Life is busy

Yeah, you reckon, Lorraine?! The simple fact is that the couple of generations of women (let's say women aged 20–60) who are likely reading this book are taking on a shit-ton more than their mothers or grandmothers ever did.

I am all for the equality movement – for working mothers, for nurturing the different facets of women's lives. However, these new opportunities have irrefutably put women under immense pressure.

The fact is that most women I know live with a daily conflict of priorities.

They want to soften into their romantic relationships, but feel toughened by the grind of bringing an income in. They want to explore every avenue of growth available to them, but also dream of an expanse of time with an empty calendar and nowhere to be. They want to have a successful career, and be there for their families.

Sadly, many women's daily reality is a tug of war on their energy from the various commitments in their lives. And to compound the problem, the constant switching of gears between those commitments depletes their energy even further.

Then let's add the massively increased pace of life that technology has heralded. I'm sure I'm not alone in feeling that I've sometimes got the attention span of a gnat, as I'm so used to speed-consuming snippets of content on social media, news sites and WhatsApp groups.

Life has most definitely sped up in the last two decades, and that's come at a price for our energy.

2. Our support systems are inadequate

So we're busier than ever before, but our support systems haven't expanded to accommodate that busyness.

Over thousands of years, women have typically leaned heavily on their families and communities to get through what needs to be done day to day. In fact 'interdependence' is one of our core feminine characteristics according to relationship expert John Gray.

That means that, until relatively recently, women banded together in families, neighbourhoods or broader communities to care for each other's children, cook together, bring meals to each other, trade goods and services, and even support each other's births.

In many societies today, we are likely to live a distance from our families and are therefore unable to avail ourselves of the support that they might offer. Our 'village' has been condensed down to our spouses (which, obviously, puts enormous pressure on our relationships). Any additional support in our lives most likely comes from third-party paid providers, like cleaners, day care centres and babysitters.

As I write these words, I've just done a straw poll of ten female friends here in Sydney, including me. Not one of us has our parents within a two-hour drive of where we live. Two have in-laws nearby.

This would not have happened even 50 years ago.

Some couples have done a fabulous job of making their friends 'the family they choose', and have created powerful interdependence with them. Wade and I have tried to create this – with reciprocal kids' sleepovers, monthly rituals (e.g. pizza in the park on the last Friday of the month) and pitching in to help friends move house. And that's been an enormous blessing.

However, there are things that I just wouldn't ask of our friends that I would ask of family – simply because our friends' own plates are already full. Having Lexi stay over for more than one night, for example, or placing an SOS call to look after her because she's sick and Wade and I both have important work commitments that day – these are things that my sister back home in Ireland, surrounded by family, wouldn't think twice about asking.

This shift in the structure of our support systems means that a) day-to-day life feels infinitely busier, and b) many of us are operating in the knowledge that when the wheels inevitably fall off the wagon, there isn't the support to accommodate them . . . and the constant, invisible stress that the lack of a safety net carries with it.

3. Social media has warped our standards

Let me be clear here: I love social media. It's given me a platform to create a beautiful community, and I've built two businesses leveraging its power. It enables me to stay in touch with friends and family all over the world, and to access the genius of my heroines and heroes.

However, it has also propagated totally unrealistic standards for those of us who consume it.

Tuning into our gorgeous, heavily filtered Instagram feeds, we're exposed to women who have magically mastered preparing divinely delicious, superfood-driven meals, are maintaining 10/10 bodies, have perfect and photogenic relationships with their partners, or, if they have kids, are seamlessly navigating the perils of parenting – oh, and are leading their own business empires.

This then makes us question our achievements – indeed, our entire existence. If we're not achieving on a grand scale ourselves, we immediately feel useless and unworthy. We then compensate for this sense of underachieving by overachieving, and trying to emulate the standards of the influencers we follow on Instagram.

And that shit takes a LOT of time and a LOT of energy!

4. The mental load is real

In my third book, *Baby, You're Remarkable,* I talked about the Mental Load – a concept that was new to many of my readers.

Here's the nutshell version . . .

Very often women shoulder the mental load of running a household, relationship and family. Men proclaim their willingness to help with the actual execution of tasks, but they essentially spend most of their time awaiting instructions on what those tasks should be.

For most women, this means that they are the 'brains trust' of everything, from nutrition to play dates, from household repairs to supplier payments, from wardrobe updates to medical checks, from social calendars to house cleanliness (who keeps track of when the sheets were last washed?).

Equally, most women live with the knowledge that there is no backup – that if they don't remember to pay the cleaner/change Saturday's dinner plans/buy Johnny new shoes, then no-one will.

We often talk about the Mental Load as the domain of mothers, however I believe it starts much earlier than that. I know that, years before Lexi came on the scene, I seemed to absorb by osmosis Christmas gift-buying for Wade's family. I'd grown up seeing my mother as the key present buyer, and I also wanted to forge ties with his family.

There are numerous ways in which carrying the Mental Load has a negative impact on a woman's life. Resentment of her partner and the ensuing relationship difficulties that that creates, for sure. A mental To Do list that wakes her up at 3 am. The constant low-grade worry that she's forgetting something, because there's no-one else who will remember it if she doesn't.

But the biggest impact is mental exhaustion. In my opinion, the greatest cost of all is the time, headspace and energy being consumed by keeping track of all the moving parts of a household.

In my role as a business mentor, I talk a lot about 'opportunity cost'. With the Mental Load, the opportunity cost is a hefty one. It steals focus from the things that actually *do* light us up and move us forward in life – from agenda-free play time with our kids, to going the extra mile on a business project we're leading that puts us right in line of sight for that next promotion.

And yep, it decimates our energy.

5. Emotional labour is invisible work for women

I first came across the concept of 'emotional labour' in Gemma Hartley's book *Fed Up: Emotional labor, women, and the way forward.* I recently shared the idea with a retreat group, and to say that there were light bulbs going on all around the table would be an understatement.

So what *is* emotional labour?

It's a special skill that women are conditioned from a young age to possess: using our own emotional energy to persuade others to do what we need/want them to do. The net effect is that, as adult women, we expend much more energy than our male counterparts on emotional labour.

We agonise over the right words, tone and time to discuss issues with others. We triple-check emails to ensure that they're hitting the right note . . . then get our colleagues to triple-check them again just in case. Pasting on a happy face and an upbeat tone comes as second nature in order to 'rub along well' with the people around us.

I know that I feel the responsibility of emotional labour heavily in my role as a parent. I cajole, persuade, distract, deflect and employ numerous other techniques in order to get Lexi to do what I want her to do. And I don't just do it with Lexi; I do it with grown-ups too.

Wade doesn't do this — or hardly at all. When I see him in action, he's just saying it like it is, with some (but limited) regard for how his words or delivery will be perceived by others. It all looks incredibly freeing!

I truly believe that a hidden factor in so many women's low energy is that they're invisibly 'leaking' energy in the energetic massaging of others that comes with the day-to-day interactions they have.

So let's agree that, for the majority of women, there's a lot going on, yes?

FROM OVERWHELMED TO ORGANISED

I have written an entire book on getting organised – my second book, *Get Remarkably Organised* – so I suggest you check that out if you'd like to learn my full organisational methodology. But right now I want to share with you the strategies I use myself when I'm slipping into overwhelm that put me in an infinitely more optimistic and energised state of mind. There are seven of them, and here they are:

1. Get it all down on paper

The first thing is to do a full brain dump of everything that's cluttering up space in your mind. I'm talking about all those 'must remember to do X' thoughts.

Now here's the thing: what's draining isn't necessarily the task that needs doing. Where the true drain comes from is the constant looping thought telling us we must remember to complete said task – taking up mental bandwidth that we could be using elsewhere.

So the very first thing we're going to do is get all our cluttering thoughts down on paper. And we're going to use ten headings to structure the brain dump.

Here's what you need to do:

1. Go to a blank page in your notebook (A4 is ideal).
2. Create ten sections and assign one of these titles to each of the sections: Home, Work, Partner, Family, Finance, Social, Admin, Personal Grooming, Communication, Health.
3. Under each heading, dump everything that's bubbling in your mind. Get it all down, even – especially! – those tasks that you tell yourself aren't even worth writing down as they're so tiny.
4. Pick just three tasks from anywhere on the page that you'll complete this week – or, even better, today. Go with the ones that are frustrating you most.
5. Get them done and enjoy the deep satisfaction of taking another step out of overwhelm.
6. Go back to the page and pick off another three tasks . . . and so on.

Now I know that this seems freakishly simple, but it's actually a powerful tool.

First off, it makes us crystallise our thinking and do a mental purge onto paper. Once it's on paper, the tasks feel more tangible and accessible – we're now dealing with a solid object rather than thoughts floating around in our heads.

Choosing just three tasks makes it easy to get started, and completing the tasks generates momentum: you'll want to keep going with another batch – and it becomes a self-sustaining cycle.

To make it simple for you, I've included a Ditch the Overwhelm worksheet in my Step Into You Playbook to help you get your thoughts on paper – you can download the playbook for free at my website: lorrainemurphy.com.au/playbook.

2. Accept that it'll never all get done

This might sound like weird advice from someone who would be considered a productivity expert, however I believe passionately that to aim for having a totally ticked-off To Do list is unrealistic.

The fact is that I could spend all day powering through a list like the one I've just suggested you make. I'd go to bed feeling proud and fulfilled. The next morning, a whole new list would start to form (just like a constantly filling laundry basket) and so on it would go.

The realisation that I'll never *truly* get everything on every list done has been a liberating one for me. It means that I do what I can do on the day required, and this eases the stress if I don't clear the entire list.

When we're in overwhelm mode we believe that we must get all of the things done all of the time – and that the time and energy required to do that is beyond our capacity at that point. We then get caught up in inertia, and don't even try to begin.

Give yourself a permission slip to not get everything done – and then do what you can. I guarantee it'll be a productive strategy, as contradictory as it sounds!

3. Ask yourself how you're sleeping

When we're tired we are significantly more vulnerable to the perils of overwhelm. We're lacking energy, our thoughts are foggy and we are more emotional than we would be if we were our fully-rested selves. We find it harder than normal to make decisions, and we procrastinate more. We're also more likely to prop ourselves up with caffeine and sugar, which in turn messes with our natural energy levels by getting us into a high/crash/high/crash cycle.

We feel overwhelmed during the day, wake at 3 am stressing about everything we need to do, and that secures us another night of crappy sleep. Then we repeat the whole process the next day, gradually getting more and more overwhelmed and more and more tired.

As part of our mission to shift you out of overwhelm, have an honest look at how your sleep is right now and ask yourself these questions that sleep educator Lisa Maltman shared with me:

- Do you feel you are getting enough sleep?
- If not, what is stopping you from getting the recommended hours of sleep?
- How does it make you feel when you get sufficient sleep?
- What would motivate you to improve your sleep?

If it's clear to you that sleep is an issue, apply some brainpower to what actions might help you get more rest. For example:

- Is it knocking off work earlier in the evening so you can wind down for an hour before bedtime?
- Is it reading instead of watching Netflix to chill out?
- Is it getting to bed even 30 minutes earlier?
- Is it limiting your phone use at night so your brain can switch into sleep mode easier?
- Is it buying some PJs you love wearing to make bedtime more special?
- Is it having acupuncture or another alternative therapy to help you rest?

- Is it investing time and money into sleep training for your kids so the whole family can sleep through the night?

I promise you, even a 10 per cent increase in the quality and quantity of your sleep will give you an edge on getting out of overwhelm.

4. Don't wait to rest until it's all done

Oh, I am VERY good at this myself! We get our children down to bed and then I tell myself that I'll hit the sofa once 'everything is done'. I tidy the kitchen, get back to some messages, put some laundry in to soak, sort out a pile of clutter in my office, get back to some more messages . . . and all of a sudden it's 9 pm and too late to do anything significant to chill out.

I could seriously learn so much from Wade on this one. He can 'check into Rancho Relaxo' (as he puts it), regardless of whether there's laundry to be put away, dishes to be washed or admin to be addressed.

I don't think it's a coincidence that I pitch headfirst into overwhelm mode approximately 500 per cent more than he ever does. He's pacing himself by taking windows of chill time when he can – essentially insuring himself against overwhelm in future.

Disciplining ourselves to take these windows of rest also prevents us from living out a fallacy: that is, that one day it'll all be done. As I've already mentioned in this chapter, IT WILL NEVER ALL BE DONE! So to see out our lives in the pointless pursuit of creating a 100 per cent clear To Do list is setting ourselves up for abject failure . . . every single day.

5. Close the loop

Most of us will be familiar with the feeling that our brains are constantly in overdrive. Rachel MacDonald once shared on Instagram a request for people to 'close the loop' . . . that is, to get back to people who are waiting for a response from you.

From dinner invitations to speaking invitations, from kids' play dates to enquiries about the Gumtree ad you posted, we can all close the loops we're responsible for. Once you've got back to that person, the loop is closed for them both mentally and energetically. Now they can make plans (if you expressed interest) or move on (if you're not interested).

One way to ease out of overwhelm mode is to close some of these loops . . . today, if possible! When I first came across Rach's concept, I immediately thought of three loops that I'd been sitting on: 1) the need to reply to a friend who'd asked me about going to a new yoga class with her, 2) getting back to a woman I'd discussed a role with six weeks ago, and 3) responding to a request for mentoring.

By closing these loops, we create positive karma – and we'll find that people start to close loops for us, too. We might get word back on a job we applied for months ago, get a 'yes' from a client enquiry we thought was dead in the water, or get resolution on a paperwork issue that's been dragging on.

What three loops could you close today, and buy yourself back that small piece of mental real estate?

6. Defer some decisions

Attempting to make too many decisions simultaneously is a sure-fire way to park yourself indefinitely in Overwhelm Hell.

From whether or not to move states, to whether or not to swap jobs, to whether or not to start a family, our brains can have a huge number of tabs open – and, having been there myself, I can tell you it's a crazy-making place to be.

When I'm working with a decision-fatigued mentee, I try to help them close some of those tabs. I need to be really clear on this: the intent isn't for the person to actually make all of those decisions; the job at hand is to decide which decisions are urgent and which ones can be deferred.

Deferring decisions is something Wade introduced me to. It's pretty simple: we pick a future date on which we will make that decision.

I'll give you an example . . .

One of my mentees and her wife had a two-year-old son. They wanted to have another baby, but as they both worked in industries that currently had uncertain job security, it felt like a tricky time to be making such a momentous decision. Nevertheless, my mentee and her wife had been expending buckets of mental energy going back and forth on the matter of should-they-or-shouldn't-they for months now.

I explained the idea of deferring decisions to my mentee, and after our session she sat down with her wife and they both agreed that they'd make the decision two months later, when they would have some more clarity on their employment situations.

Now, this is the critical bit: you then fully park the mental roundabouts until that date.

It might seem a bit weird for me to be an advocate for this concept, given that I'm such a fan-girl of getting shit done. However, the fact is that we're not always in a position to make a decision – or we need to make one decision before we can make another one.

The super-cool thing is that deferring a decision is a decision in its own right – and you feel like you have made some progress just by deciding when you'll make it.

If you have too many mental tabs open right now, consider which decisions you could book in for a later date – and use that freed-up headspace to make the more pressing decisions.

Your brain will thank you!

7. Look after your Future Self

This was probably the most impactful principle in my book *Get Remarkably Organised*. Readers loved it because a) it's so simple to grasp, and b) it's a daily practice that they can integrate into their lives.

Our Future Self is that version of us that will exist at some point to come. It could be our Future Self tomorrow morning, our Future Self next week or our Future Self next year.

Many people live their lives pretending that their Future Self doesn't exist – and make decisions and take actions that their Future Self is not happy with them for. Examples of this are:

• leaving a cranky email until Monday morning to reply to – as our Future Self can deal with it after the weekend

- stacking the dishes in the sink rather than washing them before we go to bed – it'll be Future Self's problem when we wake up
- not packing snacks before an outing with your kids (if you have them) – hangry small people will be Future Self's concern

As you can imagine, the Future Self in each of these three scenarios is very likely to curse the Past Self for not taking the five proactive minutes it would have taken to make life easier in the future.

I try to undertake both the small and the big things that will help Future Lorraine. So, that's pulling out my gym clothes the night before, putting a yummy dinner in the slow cooker on a morning when I know my day is very full, pushing through procrastination to write the chapter I said I would so that my writing schedule doesn't fall behind . . . I could list 50 ways I do this. As well as making life feel a lot smoother, it provides me with another safeguard against potential overwhelm.

Think about what you can do to look after your Future Self. The tiniest of things can make a huge difference.

Please remember: ~~~~~~~~~~~~~~~~~

- There are many reasons why you're feeling overwhelmed, and some of them are beyond your control.
- Accepting that everything will never be completely done is liberating.
- Adequate sleep is a preventative measure from hitting overwhelm.
- Pushing yourself to the point of exhaustion is not sustainable.

- Getting your To Do list down on paper will help the mental hamster wheel to stop.
- Closing the loop with others and deciding to defer a decision will free up immeasurable mental bandwidth.
- Looking after your Future Self where possible will ease overwhelm over time.

Chapter 3

UNDERSTANDING ENERGY MANAGEMENT

OF ALL THE CHAPTERS IN THIS BOOK, THIS IS THE ONE I'VE BEEN most excited to write. As the title tells you, the chapter is about energy management. And the reason I'm so excited to write on this subject is that I believe effective, long-term energy management to be *the* most critical life skill that women can implement.

Over the last two years, the work I do with women has increasingly focused on helping them to cultivate the energy they require to be the women they want to be: to build the careers they wish to have, to be the partners, friends and mothers they wish to be, and so on.

When you think about it, every one of our achievements is fuelled by our own personal energy. And, as we talked about in the last chapter, if that energy is zapped, we have sweet FA chance of making that magic happen in our lives. We need to get to a place where we feel like we've got enough fuel in our tank, and maybe a little bit more, too, to go and create the life that we choose.

You may have a particular area of your life you'd like to improve – say, your family life, your job or your home. It might be going for that promotion at work or getting your business to the next level. Whatever it is for you, you are not going to be able to create that if you are exhausted, depleted and resentful. It just ain't happening!

It really does amaze me that we're not taught about energy management at school. Imagine a world in which every person, from an early age, was encouraged to examine exactly what builds their energy, what drains it, and how they can optimise it to get the very most out of their precious lives. It would be the difference between putting the cheapest petrol in the tank and the fancy turbo stuff!

ENERGY MANAGEMENT IS ESPECIALLY IMPORTANT FOR WOMEN

I believe that energy management is important for both men and women. However, I do think we women need to be a hell of a lot more intentional about our energy. In my experience, women find it a lot more difficult to switch off than men. Even as I'm writing these words I'm also thinking about the pancakes that Wade is cooking in the kitchen next door, about the activities I'll do with Lexi later on today, the laundry that's sitting in the machine waiting to be hung out, that business proposal I emailed to someone yesterday and the birthday card I want to send to a BFF this afternoon. And that's not even half of it! This just seems to be my default setting – amiright ladies?

In a session with relationship therapist Dr Robert Maciver, Wade and I were treated to a vivid representation of the differences between the way male and female brains appear to be structured. Robert quoted relationship expert Mark Gungor's humorous video 'A Tale of Two Brains', in which Gungor proposes that men's brains are arranged into compartmentalised boxes, each with a different label. So Wade will have a box called 'Work', one called 'Dad', as well as 'Lorraine', 'Gym', 'Motorbike', 'Mates', 'Parents', 'Books', 'Sleep' . . . and so on. He spends his days moving from one box to another but is only ever in one box at a time. If he's reading a book, he's in his Book Box. If he's riding his motorbike, he's in his Motorbike Box.

Robert then described how Gungor sees a woman's brain: a mass of interconnected wires joined to every part of her life, and every wire simultaneously live. This means that something that happens in the office at work can immediately connect to something to do with a friend, or something at home will link instantly to future holiday plans.

Now here comes the nugget that blew me away.

Apparently, the two favourite boxes for a man to be in are . . . wait for it . . . the Sex Box . . . and the Nothing Box. The Sex Box I'm able to comprehend, but I needed educating on the Nothing Box.

The Nothing Box, according to Gungor, is a special place men can visit where there's simply NOTHING GOING ON. They are not thinking about anything, they are not planning anything, they are not wondering about what they'll eat for lunch. They are simply NOWHERE! This is why men can crash out in front of the TV, aimlessly kick a football around or scroll endless YouTube reviews of a gadget.

Their special skill, however, is to do nothing even when there are dishes in the sink, a child is having a meltdown in the next room or their partner is fuming right next to them.

I was talking to my friend Claire Obeid recently, and she was expressing her amazement that, when she asks her husband Chris what he's thinking about he will say, 'Nothing'. At that same moment she might have 18 different topics live in her mind!

The fact that we women haven't been blessed with a Nothing Box is precisely why I believe that schooling ourselves on how to best manage our energy is more critical for us than it is for the men around us.

THE CAPITAL VERSUS INTEREST ENERGY MODEL

I first read about energy in terms of capital and interest in Mason Currey's *Daily Rituals: Women at work*. Currey quotes American soprano Leontyne Price explaining how demanding her opera performances were and how she'd need a day after to recuperate because, in her words, 'I much prefer to sing on my interest than my capital'. This idea really resonated with me.

Now, when I kick-start any energy management discussion with the women I work with, here's what I say first: Think about your energy as a savings account. You've got X amount of money in that bank account, aka your capital. Each month you earn interest on that capital. To be in a really strong financial position, you'd ideally only spend your interest, leaving your capital nest egg intact. It's the very same for your energy!

If you can create a situation whereby you're protecting your energy capital, and only 'trading' the interest, you'll be living a life where there's plenty of energy to go around for all the people and commitments you want to devote it to.

The problem I see with a lot of women, however, is that they've run out of interest and are into their capital energy . . . and for some, that capital is about to run out. Running out of capital is energy bankruptcy. When it occurs, that's when you have burnout, with all its associated shittiness and stress.

IDENTIFYING YOUR ENERGY BOOSTS AND ENERGY LEAKS

When I'm working with women to help them understand their personal energy management, I also talk about buckets.

'*Buckets*?!' I hear you exclaim.

Let me explain . . .

You can fill a bucket right up to the top with water. However, if there are holes in that bucket, the water is going to escape – quickly if those holes are big, slowly if the holes are tiny.

Your energy is the very same. There is no point in having 'Self-care Sunday' each week if the days from Monday to Saturday are the equivalent of coin-sized holes in the bottom of your bucket. You can undertake endless activities to fill that bucket up, but that water is coming straight back out again! These are what I call 'energy leaks' – and they're lethal.

I separate these boosts and leaks into two camps each: *major boosts and minor boosts;* and *major leaks and minor leaks.* To help you differentiate, I've created the following tables using responses from mentees and program participants I've worked with over the years.

Major energy boosts	Minor energy boosts
• a holiday • a positive change – new job/home/ relationship • resolving a major energy leak • a great date and/or sex with a romantic partner • soul chats with a close friend • fun family time • achieving a goal • a self-awareness breakthrough	• a great night's sleep • a long shower or bath • a blow-dry • the perfect hot drink • massage/acupuncture/ bodywork • exercise • time to read • a hug
Major energy leaks	**Minor energy leaks**
• ongoing relationship challenges – with a partner, parents or friends • unhappiness with work • financial stress • significant health problems – ourselves or others • grief • ongoing dissatisfaction with health/ weight/appearance • extended sleep deprivation or disruption • frustration with our physical space (home or office)	• a bad night's sleep • an overloaded email inbox • an argument with a friend or partner • unnecessary noise • boring/monotonous tasks • feeling gross after eating food that doesn't work for your body • household mess • being distracted during focused tasks

Here are some personal examples from one month of my life:

My major energy boosts	My minor energy boosts
• starting this book • a 24-hour visit to friends on the coast • Lexi going back to school after a week off sick • having two girlfriends over for an intimate ladies' dinner party	• getting my hair done • a strong yoga class • replacing our old dinnerware with a gorgeous new set • a bushwalk in a new area
My major energy leaks	My minor energy leaks
• a family argument • Lexi being off school for a week with hand, foot and mouth • the associated sleep deprivation • emotional disconnection with Wade due to his work stress and intense co-parenting during Lexi's week of illness	• feeling behind with responding to emails and text messages • past-their-prime eyelash extensions that I need to get removed • Lexi challenging boundaries • noise from the renovation across the street

To help you identify what boosts and drains your own energy, I've included a worksheet in my free Step Into You Playbook for you to download from my website (lorrainemurphy.com.au/playbook).

Here's how it works . . .

1. You'll see that the worksheet has a bucket graphic on it – this represents your energy day to day.
2. The top half of the bucket represents what *boosts* your energy – the top left quadrant is for *major boosts* and the top right quadrant is for *minor boosts*.

3. The bottom half of the bucket represents what *leaks* your energy – the bottom left quadrant is for *major leaks* and the bottom right quadrant is for *minor leaks*.

4. What I'd like you to do is to spend some time reflecting on your energy *right now* – not that day last week when you felt fabulous, or yesterday when you felt really crap. This is a snapshot in time today, and you can come back to this exercise as many times as you like.

5. Work through the four quadrants, noting what your major energy boosts, minor energy boosts, major energy leaks and minor energy leaks are.

IMPORTANT NOTE

This exercise can be confronting – I know it is for me! The key thing to remember is that growth and change cannot come without self-awareness, and the name of the game with this exercise is self-awareness.

Now that you have a handle on your energy right now, let's move on to what we can do to help you max out the energy in your life, day to day.

INTROVERTS AND EXTROVERTS

We're all familiar with the idea that on one end of the spectrum are the true-blue introverts and on the other end are the raging extroverts.

Now, I need to bust some myths here. What we have been led to believe is that introverts are shy, socially awkward and retiring beings, and that extroverts are loud, socially confident and always the life and soul of the party. The difference between the two *actually* is that *introverts gain energy from time alone* and *extroverts gain energy from time with others.*

This information is critical to successfully managing your energy day to day. If you're an introvert living life on an extrovert's terms, you'll be exhausting your energy constantly. And if you're an extrovert living an introvert's life, you'll feel constantly drained.

So, how do you know which one you are?

Quiz: Are you an introvert or extrovert?

Q. YOU'RE PLANNING A NIGHT OUT, WHICH OPTION SOUNDS MORE FUN?

a   Going out with a group of friends – the more people around the more fun you have.

b   Dinner with your best friend, just the two of you sharing what's on your minds.

Q. IF YOU HAD TO CHOOSE ONE, WHICH WOULD YOU PREFER?

a   A weekend packed with social plans.

b   A weekend with zero social plans.

Q. IN GENERAL AFTER ATTENDING A LARGE PARTY OR NETWORKING EVENT, HOW DO YOU FEEL?

a   Energised and ready for more.

b   Tired and drained, even if you had fun.

Q. HOW DO YOU FEEL ABOUT MEETING NEW PEOPLE?

a It's exciting and interesting.

b It's tiring and a little nerve-racking.

Q. YOU FIND YOURSELF HOME ALONE FOR THE AFTERNOON, WHAT'S YOUR REACTION?

a Restless, so you call a friend to chat.

b Thrilled you finally got a few hours all to yourself.

Q. IF YOU HAD TO CHOOSE ONE HOLIDAY, WHICH WOULD IT BE?

a A cruise where there are lots of things to do and people to meet.

b A warm beach and a book, either alone or with one other person.

Q. WHEN YOU SEE A FREE NIGHT IN YOUR CALENDAR, WHAT DO YOU DO?

a Immediately book in a social engagement or date night.

b Look forward to a quiet evening at home.

If you got mostly As, it's highly likely you're an extrovert; mostly Bs and it's highly likely you're an introvert. Some people display both introvert and extrovert tendencies – they're called ambiverts (also known as omniverts). If you got roughly the same number of As and Bs, chances are you're one of those unicorns, and you might find the information from both of the following sections resonates with you.

Energy management for introverts

I'm mentoring a woman at the moment who owns a very successful day spa – appointments are booked out for months in advance.

She's been so 'in' the business (i.e. seeing clients) that she hasn't had time to be 'on' the business (i.e. hiring more beauty therapists to deal with demand).

At our first session, she was *wiped*. Remember when we talked about capital versus interest? Well, this woman had burned through her interest, her capital . . . and was in an energy overdraft.

During our session I asked some questions to determine whether she was an introvert or extrovert . . . and could tell very quickly that she was most definitely an introvert. The problem with her role was that she was with people all the time – 60 or more hours a week dealing one-on-one with clients, and then there was the team management of a busy day spa.

In telling me about her week, the only time she looked energised was when she told me that on Sundays – when the spa was closed – she would go in and potter about tidying up and caring for the plants.

When I put forward the idea that she was constantly working against her natural introvert tendencies, she had a huge a-ha! moment. How could she possibly feel energised when her entire working week was effectively working against her?

So, what can introverts who need to be 'on' with people do to manage their energy? The answer lies in 'restorative niches'. I learned about these little pockets of magic from Susan Cain's revolutionary (for me, anyway!) book *Quiet: The power of introverts in a world that can't stop talking*. Often an introvert just needs a small window of time alone to charge themselves up before going back into situations featuring other people. Most introverts know how to do this from an early age, but they get conditioned to ignore their own energetic pulls by people-pleasing and not wanting to be the odd one out.

I saw this recently with our daughter Lexi, who shows all the signs of being an introvert, when she had her best buddy Basil over for a sleepover. They played from 5 pm until bedtime at 7.30 pm, and were instantly playing as soon as they were both up the next morning. But an hour and a half later I discovered Lexi sitting solo on the floor of our home office with the door closed, writing me a card. Meanwhile Basil (the high extrovert) was searching the house for his playmate. I explained to him that Lexi needed a few minutes of space, and that she'd be out soon. He wasn't satisfied with this, and went into the office – where Lexi promptly told him rather firmly to leave her alone . . . and (clever boy) he did. She emerged about 15 minutes later and recommended playing with full energy again.

Without realising what she had done, Lexi had created a restorative niche – something I taught my day spa mentee to do during our session.

Her challenge was that once she was at the spa, she was guaranteed to have people around her – therefore we needed to build those niches into her time outside of work. So, rather than driving five minutes to get her morning coffee, three days a week she began walking the 20 minutes each way – to max out solo time. On Sundays she would go for a ride on her motorbike with her husband. Even though she was technically with someone else, she said she felt in her own world on her bike.

Energy management for extroverts

Extroverts need their time with others to charge up. If they don't get that time, they can really struggle. During the COVID-19 lockdowns you probably noticed extroverts where you didn't think there were any. All of a sudden, those who got their 'hit' from office banter found themselves stuck working from the kitchen table. I am married to one of them.

Wade is a man I would class as a raging extrovert. During lockdown, he would walk to our local cafe for a takeaway coffee to break up his morning of working at home. Even though the cafe is just a two-minute walk from our house (and their service is super-quick), it would take him at least 30 minutes to complete the mission, as he would stop for a socially-distanced chat with every other extrovert lingering outside their house on the street! He would return from his cafe adventure like a different person – super-energised, and full of neighbourhood news.

If you're an extrovert, consider your need to be with other people in order to 'charge yourself up' when you're planning your week. Spending time with others will build your energy, but even just knowing you have that time booked into your diary will be good for your mindset.

Joining groups or clubs (virtual or in person) will enable you to connect with new people, and working towards a common goal can be extra energy boosting for extroverts.

When you're collaborating on a project at work, try to create blocks of time where you can work together in real time rather than trading emails, texts or instant messages – if not in person, then over Zoom.

If you work from home, try shifting to a new environment occasionally – working at a cafe, a coworking space or even at a friend's place. The noise and incidental interactions with others will likely be more fuelling for you than constantly working at home solo.

Instigate a weekly walk or run with a friend – and make it the same day/time/place each week for ease of organising. You could also try building in conversations with friends who don't live near you into your exercise – I like to book in a chat with a friend back in Ireland during a morning walk.

Of course, like all of us, extroverts can get caught up in the busyness and overstimulation of the outside world, and disconnect from their thoughts and feelings. It's important for them to have downtime on their own to maintain a connection to themselves. But don't be caught in the trap of thinking you're having alone time if you're by yourself yet mindlessly scrolling Instagram or Facebook. And equally, don't rely on that scrolling to tick your 'interaction with others' box – real-time conversations with people will be a lot more energising that social media exchanges.

Please remember:

- As women, we haven't been blessed with a Nothing Box, so we need to be extra intentional about our energy management.
- When you're effectively managing your energy, you're expending the *interest* from your 'energy bank account' – never your capital.
- Energy boosts build your energy and energy leaks zap it. Identifying and acting on your unique set of boosts and leaks will enable you to optimise your energy.

- Introverts gain their energy from time alone, while extroverts gain energy from interactions with others.
- Restorative niches are critical for introverts to maintain their energy.
- Scheduling time with others will give extroverts reliable windows to build their energy.

Chapter 4

MASCULINE ENERGY AND FEMININE ENERGY

OKAY, MY FRIEND, WE'RE GETTING INTO THE REALLY JUICY STUFF now! We're continuing the energy management conversation, but we're going to look at it from a second perspective. What I'm about to share with you is *the* biggest realisation I've had when it comes to my own energy management, and I've made it the cornerstone of my work for the last two years.

Have a read of these statements:

'I feel like I can never switch off.'
'I'm constantly overwhelmed.'
'I'm drained.'
'I feel sucked dry.'
'I just can't seem to get on top of my To Do list.'

'My emotions are brittle.'
'I feel wired a lot of the time.'
'I can't get motivated.'

If any of these statements sounds like you right now, you are not alone. Many women in my community express sentiments like these, and I've felt them many times in my own life.

So what's going on?

The truth is, we're stuck in our masculine energy.

From my explorations on this topic, I've learned that all of us – men and women alike – possess both masculine and feminine energy. The ideal ratio of masculine versus feminine energy will differ for each individual, but when both energies are in balance, we feel at our very best.

Here's a really simple way to explain the concept of the two energies, and why we need both. Think about a glass of water. The glass itself represents masculine energy – it's solid, structured and holds the water in place. The water is feminine energy – it's flowing and changes shape easily. Without the water, the glass is empty – it's got no soul, no substance. And without the glass, the water splashes over everything and has no direction. So we need a balance of the form and structure (masculine energy) and the flow and creativity (feminine energy). Below are more characteristics of each type of energy.

Masculine energy: *structure, focus, direction, solidness, consistency, steadiness, control, hustle, 'make it happen', pushing, facts, logistics, thinking, operating from the neck up*

Feminine energy: *creativity, flow, trust, calm, nurturing, receiving, manifesting, intuition, feelings, being, operating from the neck down ('gut instinct')*

You don't need me to tell you that we live in a go-go-go world and that constant busyness takes its toll on everyone, especially women. In order to navigate the To Do lists, deadlines and multiple (and constant) priorities of our lives, we've learned to take a 'hustle' approach to it all – essentially, we end up being in our masculine energy a LOT of the time. We're pushing, we're focused on the when/where/why and flinging ourselves headfirst into every single day to make it all happen.

Now, I am a queen of productivity and organisation (seriously – I wrote a bestselling book on it!), but I've learned the hard way that pushing/controlling/hustling too much is a one-way street to overwhelm, exhaustion, burnout and ongoing health problems.

Since intentionally exploring my feminine energy, I've created more, achieved more, made more money, softened into my marriage, been more present with our family, rediscovered my libido and found more flow in my life. And I want to teach you to do the same!

TEN STRESS SIGNS FOR WOMEN

For me, I know I'm in my masculine energy when I'm trying to control: I'm planning the weekend, I'm trying to get Lexi out the door to school, I'm filming one program or I'm designing the next program. There's a lot happening. Whereas, when I'm in my feminine energy, I'm a lot more calm and receptive to ideas and the inspiration coming my way, and I'm tuning into my intuition more.

This is not to say that my feminine is better than my masculine or that my masculine is better than my feminine – I need a balance of both energies in my life to do what I want to do.

You need a balance of both, too, but what happens for us women when we start to tip into overwhelm mode is that we get stuck in our masculine, addicted to that 'always on' energy. The more we push, the more we find it difficult to get back into a state of feminine energy.

This is a real, burning issue for women right now. I see it every day in my work.

John Gray, author of the infamous relationship guide *Men Are from Mars, Women Are from Venus*, explores the idea of being stuck in your masculine energy in his most recent book, *Beyond Mars and Venus*. Coming to this guide 25 years after the original I was keen to find out what Gray thought of the roles in heterosexual relationships today. His take on how deeper love can be found when each partner is able to express their unique blend of masculine and feminine energies was fascinating, but what I found most enlightening is that Gray brought home how detrimental being stuck in your masculine energy really can be.

Gray identifies ten stress signs that arise from a woman constantly operating in her masculine energy, and how these 'symptoms' worsen if she continues to stay in that masculine space. As I read the signs, I realised I was saying *'tick, tick, tick'* to each one. After you've lived through feeling constantly overwhelmed (tick!), run the negative thought cycle on repeat (tick!), and just generally got to a place where you're both exhausted all the time and can't sleep (tick and tick!), Gray says that you've set yourself up for the much more detrimental symptoms of mental inflexibility, resistance to change and finally – and most concerning of all – depression. This rang so true that I really sat up and took notice.

I know that for many women reading this book, these stress signs might be mega-confronting, but please don't panic. You're in the right place, and we're here to work on this together.

So . . . what can we do about this?

IDENTIFY WHICH ENERGY YOU'RE IN

First off, how do you know what energy you're in at any one time? Bearing in mind that this will differ for each of us, here's a general guide.

If you're in your masculine energy, you'll be:

- focused on achieving an outcome (from getting your teenager off their phone to finishing a report for your Friday-morning meeting)
- rattling through a batch of logistics (maybe packing for a holiday or work trip)
- firmly plugged into your thinking mind (for example, while calculating how/what/when you're going to get tasks done or make the multiple commitments on Saturday morning work together)

If you're in your feminine energy, you'll be:

- feeling calm and comforted (maybe after a long chat with a friend where you shared a problem and felt reassured by them)

- experiencing a sense of spaciousness around whatever activities you're engaged in (perhaps being able to switch off and flow in a yoga class)
- feeling like you're 'in' your body (like the deep relaxation after a bath or massage)

Remember, we need a balance of both energies – neither is good or bad! As I've already said, for women the challenge arises when we're operating too much in our masculine energy and not giving ourselves the opportunity to drop into a feminine space.

IMPORTANT NOTE

I mistakenly bought into the idea that mothering is pure, loving and nurturing, and that me in Mama Mode would automatically have me in my feminine energy. Eh, *no*!

What I actually learned is that 80 per cent of being a mother is pure hustle. It's a non-stop list of Shit To Do, all the while anticipating the needs of a smaller human.

They're awake? Okay, what do we feed them? They're crying? Okay, is it hunger, tiredness, teething, the need for attention or a mix of all four? They're in bed for the night? Okay, what needs to be done to reduce stress as much as possible in the morning? Then, when children get older there's another whole set of concerns to address. They had an argument with their best friend at school? Okay, how do we approach it in a way that supports them right now and ensures they don't grow up to be a psychopath/bully/victim/anxious mess?

The cuddles, the giggles, that knock-you-sideways bond – that sweet, calm, nurturing 20 per cent portion of parenting comes hand in hand with the other, hustling 80 per cent.

Now that you've got more of an understanding of both types of energy, let's explore some strategies you can use to transition back to that feminine energy more.

TEN WAYS TO ACCESS YOUR FEMININE ENERGY

Once you've identified that you're veering too much into your masculine energy, the next step is to choose a way to shift yourself back into your feminine. Enter stage left my feminine energy 'toolkit': ten of the best ways I've discovered to transition myself back into my feminine with ease and grace.

1. Have sex

We're going to speak a lot more about sex in Chapter 15, but it needs a serious hat-tip in this list as well! Sex is a brilliant way for women to get into their feminine energy, and for men to get into their masculine energy. When a woman has sex, it's her body doing all the things that a woman does in order to find space and enjoyment – and, critically, to be receptive of that pleasure. Likewise for men.

John Gray references the fact that when, as a therapist, he was counselling heterosexual couples, he would rarely find that they were having what they considered to be adequate sex. His theory is that couples are a lot more likely to have happy relationships if they're having sex, as the woman is secure in her feminine energy and the man is secure in his masculine energy.

I can vouch for this theory in my relationship. If for Wade and me it's been too long between intimate encounters, the bickering and general grating on each other's nerves increases tenfold. We make love and it's like a magic wand has been waved over our entire household!

I need to be really clear here: sex does not have to be with someone else to get that hit of calming feminine energy. Self-pleasure is a brilliant way to access it, too.

2. Get into, or near, water

Remember the water glass example, when I talked about the masculine energy being the glass and the feminine energy the water? Feminine energy is intuitive, it flows and is inherently fluid, and water is a physical manifestation of these characteristics.

As a result, anything you can do with water is going to really help you tap into your feminine energy. This could be an hour-long bath, or even a five-minute shower. I can be dropped straight into my feminine energy after five minutes under running water, so if I've got a very masculine day ahead, I'll schedule in a shower at the end of it – one that I can take my time with. You could also go for a walk by water, if you're lucky enough to live by a beach, bay, river or lake. And of course, swimming is wonderful too.

3. Enjoy adornment

Adornment is anything that makes us look and feel nice – and women have been adorning themselves for thousands of years. My ultimate adornment is having my hair blow-dried, but for you it might be having your lashes, nails or eyebrows done. It might be wearing your favourite vintage dress, or that red lipstick you love. The motivation here is *not* impressing others, or trying to land a date on Friday night. It's about you and helping you feel like you're in your feminine energy.

An easy win for many women I've worked with has come from wearing dresses more often. When I think of my standard day, I'll spend a portion of it in activewear leggings, and likely another portion in jeans or shorts. Dresses, for whatever reason, tend to be for 'special' days. Putting on a dress in the morning rather than my go-to jeans instantly puts me more in my feminine energy.

One of my long-time mentees, Margaret, works in a male-orientated industry, running a business with her husband. She's a mum of three teenage boys and spends much of her time outside of work watching rugby matches. After hearing me out on the subject of finding one's feminine energy, she invested in some softer dresses – and I can tell you first-hand how much I can see her energy shift when she wears one of them.

4. Talk to a close girlfriend

Female bonds are so important. Unfortunately for many of us, when life gets busy, time with our girlfriends is the first thing to drop off the agenda. I can feel the benefit on a physiological level when I'm having a really good chat with a friend. It's like every cell is awake in my body – and that's because I'm getting myself back into that feminine space.

5. Enjoy little luxuries

Little luxuries include having a slightly fancier tea than you'd usually buy, using some nicer-than-normal shampoo, or treating yourself to regular Clean Sheet Days (something I swear Wade has never once noticed in the 12 years we've been together!). I also love using my magnesium spray and body lotion after a bath or shower, and putting on my favourite pyjamas. These small indulgences help us to feel special, nurtured and cared for – all key feelings for us to access our feminine energy.

6. Meditate

The antithesis of rushing (a very masculine energy activity) is to stop and be mindful, whether that's 60 seconds of conscious breathing or 20 minutes of Vedic meditation. If you're new to meditation, I recommend an app called Insight Timer, which has thousands of guided meditations. And remember that meditation doesn't *need* to involve sitting cross-legged and reciting mantras – many women I know undertake moving meditation, which they do while walking, swimming or even cooking.

7. Exercise

Anything that gets us into our neck-down area is a good thing for getting into our feminine energy. Gentle exercises like yoga, walking and Pilates are better for fostering the flow of feminine energy than full-on HIIT classes, however the exercise you choose needs to work for you!

8. Get into nature

Think about Mother Nature. We typically think of her as wild and free – she does whatever she wants. Any way we can connect with the natural world will help us transition into a feminine energy space. You might live near a beach or park, or you might be able to explore a local bushwalk, but even just getting outside will help.

We have a tiny garden but it's packed full of plants, and I love having my lunch amongst them. Or I'll go for an eight-minute walk around the block, which takes me through our local park, to break up my work day. Even the tiniest sips of nature can really help us get back to our centre when we've been running hard on masculine energy.

9. Harness the power of essential oils

I love essential oils as a way to connect to my senses and transition myself into a feminine space where I'm feeling more grounded in my body. Rose, lavender, geranium, ylang-ylang, frankincense and sweet orange essential oils are my favourite helpers to access my feminine energy. We have an oil diffuser in our bedroom and I'll have these oils diffusing at bedtime to really drop into a softer energy. I also have them near my desk if I find myself getting too much into that masculine hustle mode during my working day.

10. Treat yourself to some pampering

Treating yourself to anything that helps you feel nurtured, safe and cared for is an amazing way to tap into your feminine energy, especially something involving touch (like a massage). Reflexology, a facial or acupuncture could work if you want to go to an expert, or try a soothing Epsom salts bath or at-home manicure if you're staying at home.

IMPORTANT NOTE

There is a very powerful physiological hack that John Gray introduces in *Beyond Mars and Venus* that I want to share with you here. You're probably familiar with the hormone oxytocin – aka 'the love hormone'. It's what we produce when we experience affection, when we're feeling supported . . . and when we're engaging in something that places us in our feminine energy (hint: consult the list I've just shared with you!).

When a woman creates more oxytocin, it reduces her testosterone and her body can then produce more oestrogen. Oestrogen is one of our two core feminine hormones (the other being progesterone). Oestrogen calms us and reduces stress. So the more we do these feminine-energy-enhancing activities, the more we produce oxytocin, lower our testosterone and increase our oestrogen – which means we can calm the farm more!

Now, here's something really, really important. Are you listening?

John Gray explains that a woman's body doesn't start creating oxytocin when she's having an experience (a date night, a massage, a long shower). *It starts creating it as soon as she knows that experience is going to happen!*

For example, you book a massage for Saturday afternoon. As soon as you hang up the phone from making that appointment, your body starts to create more oxytocin. How cool is that?!

This is why it's so important that we get planned and proactive about incorporating elements of this feminine energy toolkit into our lives.

A MORE FEMININE-ENERGY YOU *IS* POSSIBLE

As someone who spent *years* jammed firmly in her masculine, I want you to believe me when I say that life doesn't have to feel so tough. A more peaceful, less stressed, more 'flow-y' you *is* within you. It's not impossible to find her, no matter what your life situation might be.

As I've said a couple of times in this book already, awareness is key. Remember Maya Angelou's idea about doing better once we know better? Take the tiniest actions to start bringing some change into your life, no more. I know myself that the smallest changes done consistently have the most epic overall impact in my life.

And lastly, please have this conversation – talk to your girlfriends, your partner, your sister, your daughter. Together, let's get these ideas out into the world so that more women can release themselves from the stress symptoms that go hand in hand with losing touch with their feminine energy.

Please remember: ~~~~~~~~~~~~~

- All men and women possess both masculine and feminine energy – and we need a balance of both.
- When we're in our masculine energy, we feel we're controlling a specific outcome.
- When we're in our feminine energy, we're going with the flow.
- Understanding which energy you're in at any one point will help you tune into managing your energy.
- A major issue for many women is that they become stuck in their masculine, but there are several tools you can lean on to help you transition to a more feminine energy.
- Women need oxytocin to create more oestrogen (which calms and reduces stress) and just knowing that you have a nurturing activity coming up will help your body produce more oxytocin.

Chapter 5

FILLING YOUR TANK

OKAY, I'M CLIMBING UP ONTO MY SOAPBOX TO MAKE A VERY impassioned argument for something that drives me crazy: the term 'self-care'.

This term has exploded in recent years, and with it a flourishing industry built on helping women feel like they've ticked a box by buying products that purportedly keep them safe from burnout.

Three reasons I hate self-care, in the commercial sense of the term, are:

1. **It can set unrealistic expectations.** To me, 'self-care' represents a bath bomb purchased in the hope that, one day, we'll put it to use – and that after our immersion in the fizzy, floral-scented, petal-scattering magic, all our challenges will have floated away and we will feel reborn and ready to take on the world again.

There is an entire industry built upon setting women up with these expectations – meaning they can spend money on expensive items, and then compound the stress they're already feeling with guilt, because they're not using said items.

2. **It's optional.** The whole idea of self-care suggests that it's something we can choose or not choose to do – and that the ultimate consequences of us not doing the said caring aren't that bad . . . really.

3. **It puts women under (even more) pressure.** When I've spoken to women about the idea of self-care in their lives, they generally get a look of guilt, failure and/or panic in their eyes. This is because, on top of all the other things they're expected to do (for themselves and others), self-care is yet another item on their To Do list that tends to be ticked off last . . . if it gets ticked off at all.

Self-care just won't cut it. We urgently need to reframe how we approach caring for our energy, and how we think about that energy. And the best way I've found is to visualise your energy reserves like the tank of fuel in your car.

DRIVING ON AN EMPTY TANK

Let me tell you a little tale. I was once driving back from a speaking gig that was about three and a half hours from home. I saw a service station coming up soon after I set off, and checked the fuel gauge on my car. It was just touching the 'empty' line – so I told myself I could wait until the next service station.

The problem was . . . there wasn't another one! The red light on the fuel gauge came on, and I kept scanning the horizon for an upcoming pit stop. I was still scanning as I came to the outskirts of Sydney two hours later.

I couldn't think about anything other than the fact that the car might conk out at any minute. I was sweating, I'd turned off the podcast I was listening to, and I had many nightmare scenarios on the go simultaneously – including Lexi being stranded at day care (I was due to pick her up and Wade was away) while I was stuck in a broken down car in the middle of a busy Sydney tunnel or bridge. I can still feel the fear pulsing through my veins for every moment of that drive!

The rush of relief when I pulled up at Lexi's day care centre was epic. And miraculously the car started and made it to a service station two minutes away, once I had her safely on board.

Here's the point of this story: *too many women are living their lives in this exact way, every single day.* They're speeding through life with empty fuel tanks, hoping that somewhere, sometime, somehow they'll get a chance to stop and fill up. The problem is that that opportunity often doesn't come, and they sink into ever-greater exhaustion.

This is why I don't refer to self-care in my work – instead I state the need for women to 'fill their tanks'. Effective tank-filling means that we have the energy to go about our days with motivation, contentment and positivity. We'll be exploring how to best fill our tanks shortly, but first let's take a closer look at what can happen when we're running on empty.

RESENTMENT AND BURNOUT

During a talk at New York's cultural centre 92nd Street Y, former Yahoo! CEO Marissa Mayer once said that burnout is in fact about resentment.

This makes so much sense. What really brings us to our knees (aka burnout) is not so much physical, mental, emotional or spiritual exhaustion but the ever-building resentment about our situation. That is the ultimate undoing of the entire house of cards that our empty-tank life represents. Resentment is the secret killer of many things: energy, opportunities, relationships, health, entire futures.

Marissa was speaking specifically about work-related burnout, but what she was saying has relevance to every area of our lives.

I know, for example, that I get resentful of Lexi when she gets up unusually early and I miss out on my morning meditation. I get resentful of Wade if his work commitments prevent me from getting to my exercise classes. I get resentful of my work if I'm rushing to get a task done before I collect Lexi from school and I feel like my head is still in work mode when I'm greeting her.

The point here is this: if we're making time to properly fill our tanks, then the likelihood of us falling prey to burnout is infinitely reduced.

THE FEATHER, THE BRICK AND THE TRUCK

I've found the following idea to be one of the best I've learnt for helping me (and the people I share it with!) tune into what's really going on and to avoid heading down a one-way street to burnout.

This widely used concept goes like this: if something in our lives needs our serious attention in order to prevent burnout, then the Universe will serve us a feather. The feather is irritating and slightly uncomfortable, but we can brush it away easily.

If we ignore the feather, we then get sent a brick. The brick gives us a shock and hurts at the time, but we recover fairly quickly and – maybe after a few days – we crack on with what we were doing before it hit us.

If we ignore the brick then we get a truck. This metaphorically flattens us, and we can stay that way for weeks or even months.

I've seen this play out in my life, and the lives of others, several times.

A friend of mine was working in a high-stress tourism role. The team she worked in had recently been halved . . . and its responsibility doubled. She regularly felt overwhelmed and stressed at work (her feather), however she kept powering on.

After a time, she began to experience tension headaches (her brick).

She kept going, and . . . you guessed it – she got a truck: her femur was broken on a work-organised mountain-bike outing. This meant that she was unable to work for months and had to move out of her home and back in with her parents so they could care for her.

Literally on her back after the accident, she began to envision a career beyond her current role and dreamt up her own writing business – which she went on to create once she was well again.

As a blatant, step-by-step example of the feather/brick/truck concept at play, my friend's experience is one I have flagged with a number of mentees when I have seen that they're on the brink of receiving a brick . . . or even a truck.

MY EXPERIENCE OF BURNOUT

This might be better described as a 'slow crashout' than a 'burnout'! It happened after months of ignoring multiple feathers and bricks.

In 2017 I completely changed the business model of the company I had started five years earlier. I brought a business partner on board, became a mother for the first time, navigated some heavy family stuff and then decided to sell the business.

In 2018 I talked Wade into a tree-change move to the Gold Coast in Queensland, bought a house there, had an adventure in Bali with Lexi and then got news of a financial wipe-out due to a dodgy supplier I'd engaged years before in my first business.

I set up our new life in a new state – with Wade spending most of his time tending to his growing business in Sydney, while I tried to get a new business of my own started. After three months of living in our new home I was losing my mind with loneliness, and it was decided we'd move back to Sydney. We found a new home in a new suburb and began to set up our lives again. I flung myself into writing my third book and figuring out my second business, which operated on a totally different model to the ones I'd created previously.

In early 2019 the cracks were showing. I was emotionally and mentally exhausted. Wade and I were not in a great place. And I was beset with self-doubt and worry about making my new business work. I was also experiencing intense financial stress – because of the aftermath of the financial shock the year before, and the fact that Wade and I were both in the early start-up stage of building our separate businesses.

Around this time, we found out I was pregnant – which was happy news, but not planned. At seven weeks we saw our baby's heartbeat. Then, at the point when we thought we were 11 weeks pregnant, we heard the most heartbreaking words from the sonographer: 'I'm so sorry, your baby has passed away.' I have never cried like that in my life, and I hope I never do again.

Soon after, we found out our house had extremely bad mould – and immediately we decided we needed to get out. We saw 18 rentals in three days, and moved house within nine days of discovering the mould.

The week after we moved I got another positive pregnancy test, but lost that baby a week later. I had never actually done this before, but at that point I picked up the phone to my friend Sarah and said, 'I'm not okay'. She arrived at our place within an hour – thankfully Lexi was having a nap – and to all intents and purposes scraped me off the floor.

Sarah spent the afternoon with me and said that, after all the craziness of the previous two years, this had to be my rock bottom.

I was terrified that my mental state would adversely impact Lexi (how could it not!), and I also understood that I needed a window of stability so I could address the issues in my life. After an appointment with my psychologist and another with my GP, I got a prescription for anti-depressant medication.

A few weeks later, I had a week in Bali by myself. I knew how much a break like that would help me, however I held off booking it for the usual excuses we women find to hold ourselves back from filling our tanks. As part of the rock bottom realisation, I knew I needed time for my soul to recharge – and so I finally made it happen.

That week was so healing. The chance to sleep deeply for seven nights, to nourish my body with beautiful food and yoga, to see my favourite healers there, to have space just for *me* that wasn't about looking after anyone else . . .

One night, I went to a cacao ceremony and an evening of ecstatic dance – and danced like a lunatic. I could feel myself dancing out the rage, the injustice, the hurt, the fear, the self-doubt and I felt deeply cleansed by the end of the night. I left the venue and stood on the bridge of a little stream, and felt it was finally time to say goodbye to our two little souls – so I did.

I returned to Australia feeling like a totally different person. I was so used to having an empty tank that I'd forgotten what it was like to be my invigorated, energised self. Wade said that if that's how I came home from Bali, he'd be fully supportive of me going every single month!

Between the medication and the deep recharge in Bali, I felt strong enough to overcome the challenges in my life, and I came off the medication four months later.

With the benefit of hindsight, I can see numerous points over this two-year period where I could have stopped, taken stock, filled my tank and recalibrated. Looking back, I can also identify the feathers, the bricks and the trucks.

FEATHERS
- the daily sense that I wasn't quite 'right' – including unexplained emotional outbursts and crying

- constant business and relationship stress
- ongoing relationship issues with Wade

BRICKS

- realising the tree-change move was not a good idea
- finding out we had gotten pregnant accidentally (a happy brick, but a brick regardless)
- the extensive mould growth in our house

TRUCKS

- the financial shock in 2018
- our two miscarriages

KEYS TO FILLING YOUR TANK

Thanks to that first-hand experience of burnout, I've learned a few things about filling the tank. They are:

1. Prevention is better than cure

Waiting until your tank is running on empty before you fill it is not the way to go. Don't 'save up' your restorative time, thinking you can't fit it in now. You also don't need to starve yourself of you time for days, weeks or months in order to 'earn' a window of time for yourself. The problem with these approaches is that we can move the tank-filling time further and further back, to the point that we may not get around to it until it's too late.

What is a lot more powerful is building small, restorative activities into our daily lives. A one-hour walk by yourself to keep yourself topped up *right now* is worth far more than a day at a spa in three months' time.

Consider what achievable things you could do day to day to pre-emptively fill your tank. The number-one way to keep your tank topped up is by actively focusing on prioritising these daily needs.

2. Guilt erodes its value

If we go into energy-boosting time feeling guilty then it cancels out any potential upside to us having that time. I'm deadly serious on this.

Having a coffee date with yourself and a book, and angsting about whether or not the morning alone at the cafe makes us bad/selfish/mean/unmotherly totally diminishes the potential of us being there. Equally, arranging a walk with a friend and worrying about all the work that's not getting done while you're catching up is pointless.

This takes practice, I know, but remember that any guilt or regret about you choosing to prioritise yourself is the equivalent of taking two steps forward and one step back. And remember also that everything and everyone in your life stands to gain if you can show up as your fully-charged-up self.

3. It's an investment

It's been critical for me to see tank-filling not as an expense but as an investment. When I saw it as an expense (of time and money), I would find *all the reasons* not to enjoy it. However, when I reframed it as an investment – in all areas of my life – I suddenly found I was able to give myself permission to fill my tank.

On returning from Bali in 2019, I said that the week I had spent there was the best time I had *ever* spent on myself – and I've invested heavily in time and space for my personal development over the years. The simple reason is that that week brought me back to myself.

4. It doesn't need to cost a fortune

Reclaiming your energy does not need to mean an SOS break to Bali. There are so many ways to fill your tank that do not involve taking a sledgehammer to your bank account – which is exactly why I'm about to share a list of tank-filling activities to work with any budget. I find that women often use limited funds as an excuse not to prioritise themselves, and when we can disentangle 'tank filling' from 'expensive', then we'll be a lot better off.

30 WAYS TO FILL YOUR TANK

1. Have a hot shower and don't rush it (even better, sprinkle your favourite essential oils in the shower for a steamy aromatherapy treat).
2. Book in a date with yourself – some uninterrupted time to sit in a cafe and enjoy a coffee with a good book or magazine.
3. Plan a date with your friends, or skip the ongoing logistics and have a standing monthly dinner together.
4. Listen to music you love in the car, preferably with the volume up loud!
5. Change your sheets in the morning so you can look forward to a Clean Sheet Night later on.

6. Get out in nature – go for a bushwalk, sit by the ocean or in the local park.

7. Make your favourite tea and drink it from a fancy cup (I love using Wade's nan's china teacup and saucer).

8. Take a yoga or Pilates class.

9. Plan an overnight stay somewhere new.

10. Make love or enjoy some self-pleasure.

11. Watch a TV show or movie you love, especially one that makes you laugh out loud.

12. Bring back the written word! Send a card or letter to someone you care about.

13. Meditate (I love the Insight Timer app).

14. Go for a walk with a friend (I find conversations are so much more connected if I'm walking with the person).

15. Have a candlelit bath with beautiful bath salts or bubble bath.

16. Get creative! I know lots of women in my community fill their tanks with crafts, cross stitch, sewing and knitting, to name a few.

17. Cook or bake if you enjoy being in the kitchen. You could try a new recipe or make an old favourite from childhood.

18. Get a manicure, pedicure or massage.

19. Go for a swim.

20. Listen to an audiobook or podcast.

21. Put on a face mask and use a beautiful body moisturiser.

22. Have a nap, an early night or a sleep-in (or all three!).

23. Have a three-minute dance party for one in the kitchen.

24. Dig out a favourite or nostalgic piece from your wardrobe and wear it today.

25. Disconnect from social media for a few hours a day, or even better – turn off your phone entirely for a day.
26. Order in something delicious and treaty.
27. Take time to call a friend you haven't spoken to in a while.
28. Create a vision board (more on this in Chapter 10).
29. Buy yourself some fresh flowers.
30. Watch a TED talk.

Please remember: ~~~~~~~~~~

- Self-care is optional, filling your tank is not.
- Avoiding resentment can help us avoid burnout.
- Identifying the feathers the Universe sends us will prevent them turning into bricks or trucks.
- Saving up or deferring your tank-filling time is not in your best interest.
- Guilt will directly detract from the benefit of your tank-filling time.
- Reframe tank-filling time as an investment, rather than an expense.
- Tank-filling time doesn't need to be expensive.

Part 3

Focus on your blue-sky perspective

These chapters will step you through my goal-setting and manifesting

process, as well as help you unlock serious motivation in your life!

Chapter 6

SIMPLIFYING YOUR PURPOSE

NOW THAT YOU'VE ADDRESSED YOUR ENERGY, IT'S TIME TO START building the life that you wish to be living. And that starts with your purpose. Some call this your 'soul purpose', some call it your 'life purpose'. I'm going to go with the simple catch-all of 'purpose' for the purposes (ha!) of this chapter.

First of all, I'm going to define what this elusive 'purpose' is – and define what it is not. I'm also going to release what I see as some of the pressure points in regard to the way in which many of us are approaching the topic of purpose in our lives.

I'll share with you what I see my own personal purpose being, and the five questions I work with myself – and share with my mentees – to help them get closer to their purpose.

In the work I do with women, I talk a *lot* about purpose. And I see a lot of women get stressed about purpose.

I was fortunate to hear one of my favourite authors, Elizabeth Gilbert, speak a couple of years ago at a Business Chicks event. She articulated what I hear in the conversations I have with women on the topic of purpose. She said: 'Purpose has become an assault weapon for women to hurt themselves with.'

Ouch!

What she meant is that we women get so caught up in defining our purpose, living our purpose, staying on purpose and living a purposeful life that we get ourselves tied up in knots and actually prevent ourselves from living a life that's aligned with our purpose.

Constantly asking yourself questions like *Am I on purpose?*, *Have I found my purpose yet?*, *Is this my purpose?* is very anxiety-inducing. You might have a friend who's very clear, loud and proud on the subject of their purpose. Or you might read a book and marvel at *how bloody purposeful* the author is. I'm here to tell you that none of this is helpful! I beseech you to not treat purpose as a weighty thing. Give yourself permission to take the pressure off.

Purpose also doesn't need to be anything super-complicated or fancy. This concept has been something of a revelation for the women I've shared it with. I recently made this point on a virtual retreat I was hosting, and I could almost see the scales falling from some of the women's eyes, and the sense of relief that that brought with it.

FIRST OF ALL, WHAT PURPOSE ISN'T

One of the bugbears I have with this whole purpose thing is that the word 'purpose' has become something of an umbrella term for everything related to goal setting, life strategy, vision, mission and values . . . and this certainly doesn't ease our stress in this area! So what I'd like to explore with you now is what purpose is *not*.

I know for me, as I started to figure this whole purpose thing out, that it felt like a kind of car park for everything loosely related to life coaching or self-improvement or personal development.

Purpose is not vision

This means that your purpose is not:

- having a beautiful house
- making X dollars a year
- having a wonderful relationship with a romantic partner
- spending a month in Europe every year
- having a weekly massage
- donating X dollars to charity

All of these examples are elements of what might make up someone's vision for their life: the composite 'end state' on the other side of the daily task of bringing their Dream Life into reality, individual goal by individual goal.

If I think about my vision for my life, part of it is to be living in a five-bedroom home, close to nature, with Wade, Lexi and Wilder. This is my vision, but it's not my purpose.

Your purpose is not where you want your life to be or what you want your life to look like in the near or not-so-near future. That's your vision.

Purpose is not passion

To bring this point to life, I'll share some of my passions with you. Chocolate is one of them, for sure! And so is cooking, and pretty much anything to do with food: thinking about food, planning food, shopping for food . . . the lot.

Another passion of mine is health and wellbeing. Nourishing myself and my family, engaging in sessions with health experts, finding the right supplements for what each of us needs at any one time, learning about new health approaches – I love it.

A third passion is travel: the feeling of landing somewhere new, the sounds and smells of foreign places, the new perspectives gained by being away from home. I also love reconnecting with a place I've visited before (Bali being top of my list).

A fourth passion is reading. I relish the opportunity to learn from non-fiction books or lose myself totally in the world of fiction.

So, these are some of my passions, but they're not my purpose.

WHAT PURPOSE IS

Purpose is the North Star in our lives. It's why we do what we do, why we get out of bed in the morning, why we keep going despite obstacle after obstacle.

Purpose keeps us going in the face of whatever comes our way. No matter how easy it is on some days, how excruciatingly difficult it is on other days . . . it keeps us fuelled up and moving forward.

Simon Sinek refers to purpose as 'knowing your why'. He's done TED talks on the topic, written a book (*Start With Why*) about it, and has built his business on helping people to identify and live their 'why'.

Why do *you* get up and do what you do every day?

I see purpose as the opportunity to live and breathe whatever that North Star is in your life, every day.

YOUR PURPOSE DOES NOT *NEED* TO BE YOUR WORK

This point has resulted in more a-ha! moments from the people I have shared it with than any other pertaining to purpose. The fact is, your purpose does not have to arise from your work.

When it comes to figuring out their purpose, and living a purposeful life, the biggest pitfall for people is that they assume their purpose needs to be whatever makes them money. The reason I say it's a pitfall is that it's not going to be possible for absolutely every person to make their central purpose also be their chief way of making a living.

We have this loaded expectation of: 'Well, I need to be making money, and that money should come from my purpose. And if I'm not doing that, then I'm failing and I'm not living a purposeful life . . . and I'm an absolute disaster as a human.'

I recall one participant of a recent retreat being in tears when the realisation landed with her that her purpose didn't have to be tied up with her work. She had put so much pressure on herself to find a job that 100 per cent brought her purpose to life. She realised, as I was speaking, that she could actually very happily live her purpose more broadly in her life.

At another retreat I hosted, one of the guests, Brigid, informed the group that she had started two businesses with her partner and they were just about to start their third. It was during an exercise on vision, passion and purpose that it became clear to Brigid that her purpose was actually family. This was a huge surprise to her, and it was also a surprise to me! There were two reasons for this surprise. First, given that she had three businesses, *surely* her purpose must be related to work? And secondly, being a parent was not something she had chosen in her life. But she had nieces she was very close to, and she realised that family was her purpose.

Brigid's realisation that day was an active demonstration of the fact that we don't necessarily need our purposes to be putting dollars in the bank account every week, fortnight or month.

Your purpose might be kindness, and you bring that to life by practising more kindness in the world every day.

Or your purpose might be to spread more joy around you, by bringing a smile to others' faces.

Another purpose might be to leave places and people just that bit better than how you found them.

Your purpose is going to be as unique as a thumbprint. It's not necessarily going to make sense to your partner or your best friend or your colleague or your kids. And it doesn't need to – it's yours!

IT'S OKAY TO CHANGE YOUR MIND

Your purpose can also shift over time. Maybe you had a super-clear purpose five years ago, but life evolved in a direction that has left that purpose feeling somewhat clunky – like a pair of jeans that used to fit well but have lost their shape. This is perfectly fine. We humans are dynamic beings; we're not supposed to lock into a certain position and not move or change for the duration of our lives!

You cannot know what your future experiences will be, therefore it's really important that, when we're considering our purpose, we give ourselves flexibility, permission, compassion, kindness and understanding . . . essentially, that we do not use the assault weapon on ourselves!

Personally, my purpose has held firm for almost a decade, however it might shift in 20 years' time, two years' time or even in two months' time.

MY PURPOSE

My purpose is to help women rise even higher in their lives. That's been my North Star for years now, but it's manifested itself in different ways.

In 2012, I had just started the first talent agency for digital influencers in Australia. One way I manifested my purpose was to be an example of a successful female entrepreneur. Another way was through the income our team generated for the mostly female talent we represented. For some, the income was life-changing – getting to go on incredible overseas trips or putting their children through a particular school. For me, at the time, those results were perfectly aligned with my purpose, but they were also very isolated to my business.

When Lexi was born in 2017, I experienced a shift in how I saw my life. The business – essentially my firstborn child – was no longer the epicentre of my universe. I sold it and embarked on a new venture that focused on writing, speaking and mentoring. My purpose is now hardwired into this second business. Everything I do within it – my mentoring, retreats, online programs, membership groups, speaking, podcasting, writing this very book – is created from a place of me wanting women like you to rise even higher in their lives.

Today, however, I'm more cognisant of living my purpose both during and *outside of* my working hours.

The primary way I can live my purpose outside of the parameters of my work is through being a present, connected and intentional mother to our children – and most especially, Lexi. To give her the love and tools to be a woman who rises high in her life, and in doing so inspires other women to do the same – well that's my purpose quite literally personified!

But it can also manifest in the conversations I have with my friends, and other girls and women in my life. A few months ago, I had a powerful conversation with our 17-year-old babysitter about birth. I could see that this was a paradigm shift for her when it came to the idea of her perhaps one day giving birth, and I was thinking later on that night that it had been such a privilege to get to have that conversation with her – and to present a perspective to her on such a powerful rite of passage for women who do have children.

Even though for me my work is very aligned with my purpose – as we've discussed, it doesn't *have* to be. If your purpose is to put a smile on people's faces, day to day, you can do that – whether you're working as a barista, a zookeeper, a stay-at-home mother or a lawyer. You get to live that purpose in any way you choose to.

PREPARING TO IDENTIFY YOUR VISION, PASSIONS AND PURPOSE

I want to share an essential part of preparing to clarify your vision, passions and purpose that many of us (including me until recently) totally overlook.

A few months ago I was hosting a four-day retreat in Noosa and along for the ride I had my friend and guru Claire Obeid. She and I have been friends for 12 years. She's got a fascinatingly rich toolkit of spiritual modalities, as well as a beyond-grounded and tuned-in approach to her life and work.

Claire's role on the retreat was to be our spiritual guru-in-residence, and as part of this role she guided the group through a Miracle Morning each day – which included meditation, breathwork and yoga. Morning two was all about the heart space, and Claire had mapped out an intricate practice incorporating her different modalities and pearls of wisdom.

As she gently talked us through a heart-opening yoga pose, Claire said: *'Our hearts are where our dreams live.'* I felt a well-up of emotion when she said that – it was just so beautiful and true!

In my workshop afterwards, I guided the group through a series of exercises aimed at helping them define their vision, identify their passion and tune into their purpose.

I have never seen those answers drop in as quickly as I did that morning in Noosa. It was like all they needed was a tiny filigree key, and the answers fell out into their playbooks for them. Most of the women there said that it was the clearest they had ever felt about having a purpose, and they were completely taken aback by that.

I was thrilled to see this clarity, but I couldn't take the credit. I explained to the group that the energy work that they had moved through with Claire that morning had perfectly primed them to look within themselves for the answers they sought for their lives – they essentially had a hotline to their heart!

I witnessed first-hand that morning how important it is to ready ourselves physiologically to receive the answers we seek.

In this modern society, we spend much of our time hunched over – typing, scrolling through phones, leaning over as we eat, curling forward to feed babies, bending forward to pick up and tend to children . . . you get the picture. This hunched-over position means we close down our heart space. Rather than our chests shining out proudly, they're collapsed inwards. Claire taught us that our dreams live within our hearts, and those dreams aren't necessarily going to surface on demand if our heart spaces are deflated most of the time.

So, prime yourself. Do some deep breathing into your heart space, try some heart-opening yoga poses (a quick Google search will throw up some examples for you), and visualise your heart space opening up beautifully and expansively. If you like, you could even do a heart-opening practice. Claire has kindly shared a version of hers and you'll find it in your Step Into You Playbook, which you can download for free from: lorrainemurphy.com.au/playbook.

Five guiding questions

Now, I want to share with you the five questions that I have found to be the most powerful at delivering to me the clarity I want on my vision, passion and purpose. They're the same questions I put to my one-on-one mentees and retreat attendees.

The first question will bring you closer to your vision, the second will define your passion (or passions) and the final three tackle purpose.

QUESTION 1: *IF MY LIFE COULD LOOK ANY WAY, AND I COULD NOT FAIL, WHAT WOULD I DO?*

This is a powerful question to help you create a vision for yourself that is not hampered by your own limiting beliefs.

QUESTION 2: *WHAT ARE EXAMPLES OF DAY-TO-DAY BLISS IN MY LIFE?*

What day-to-day experiences bring you peace, contentment and gratitude? These are excellent clues to our passions.

QUESTION 3: *WHAT GETS ME EMOTIONAL?*

What issues, challenges, injustices or opportunities trigger an emotional response for you? The emotion could be furious, excited, happy, frustrated, lonely, or any emotion of your choice.

QUESTION 4: *WHEN IN MY LIFE HAVE I FELT A STRONG SENSE OF PURPOSE, AND WHY DID I FEEL THAT?*

This will be a time you felt you were really motivated, pulled or compelled by something beyond yourself. Our purpose will unlock an emotional charge, be that charge 'positive' or 'negative'.

QUESTION 5: *WHO ARE THREE PURPOSEFUL PEOPLE THAT I KNOW OF AND ADMIRE, AND WHY DO I FEEL DRAWN TO THEM?*

Remember that if there are qualities we admire in someone else, it's because they're qualities that are essentially in us − we might just want to develop them more.

IMPORTANT NOTE

The responses to these questions are going to be a work in progress for all of us – they're not questions you dash off answers to in your 20-minute coffee break. And it's likely that our responses will morph and shift over time. There are no 'right' answers!

A FINAL SUGGESTION

I hope this chapter has given you lots of ideas on how you can approach purpose in your life. Maybe a story I've shared about myself or someone else has resonated with you, or the questions I've posed have given you a solid base to begin thinking about your purpose.

However, most of all, I hope that this chapter has taken the pressure off purpose for you. Purpose is not something else for you to stress out about. This chapter was not created to give you even more 'to do'. If I know my readers like I think I do, I'm quite certain that you're very good – superb, even! – at putting pressure on yourself . . .

Please remember: ~~~~~~~~~~

- Cut yourself some slack when it comes to your purpose.
- Purpose, vision and passion are distinctly different things.
- Purpose can be the North Star of our lives.
- Your purpose does not need to be something you make a living from.
- Create the space to tune into that magical heart hotline.
- Take the time to ask yourself the powerful questions.

Chapter 7

BECOMING MOTIVATED

MOTIVATION IS SOMETHING I SEE MANY, MANY WOMEN STRUGGLING with. My intent with this chapter is to take the mystique out of motivation, so that you can move through those days (or even weeks or months) when what I call the CBF (Can't Be Fucked) Index is high.

Let's jump right in. I'm going to pack some punches here.

IT IS IMPOSSIBLE TO BE MOTIVATED WHEN YOU'RE EXHAUSTED

Motivation and exhaustion are like oil and water – they cannot be combined. So if you're feeling unmotivated, step one is to ask yourself: 'Am I exhausted?' Remember from Chapter 4 that exhaustion is, according to John Gray, one of the ten signs of stress for women stuck in their masculine energy.

Recently I went for a walk with a couple of girlfriends. One, a successful coach and entrepreneur, was talking about how knackered she was feeling. Her 13-month-old girl still hadn't nailed the sleeping-at-night gig, and on this particular week it had gotten worse because the baby was also having a rough ride with teething. My friend said she had been up eight or nine times a night. As a naturally high-energy person, she said she was really starting to feel the exhaustion kick in.

Over the course of the same walk, she also told us that she was frustrated at her lack of organisation, and that she constantly felt behind the eight ball with life admin, meal prep and 'on-the-business' work. Her default setting was a love of order and routine, and I could tell how much this current situation was getting to her.

The fact is, when we're running in exhausted mode, it's practically impossible to summon the motivation to put in the yards with your work, health, routines, parenting and so on. Our bodies, minds and souls are in survival mode – just trying to make it from one end of the day to the other. And when we heap pressure on ourselves to summon motivation from the ether, we wear ourselves out even more.

Let me give you an example from my own life.

One Monday night I had a sales campaign closing within my business, on the Tuesday night I was on a virtual group mentoring session until 9.30 pm, on the Wednesday night I worked until 10 pm getting ready to start a speaking tour, on the Thursday night I presented for three hours, and on the Friday night I (probably predictably) got a tension headache and slept horribly.

This was on top of my full work days, driving three and a half hours each way to Canberra, and Wade being away all week, so I was solo parenting and coordinating a nanny to stay over with Lexi while I was away on that Thursday night. Oh, and I was 31 weeks' pregnant at the time. Madness, really, when I look back at it!

On the Saturday I did my usual market shop, had breakfast with Wade and Lexi, and then left for a physio appointment and a prenatal yoga class. Back home, I had a two-hour window in which to pack to go away on my tour.

I can tell you, my CBF Index was through the roof! The mere thought of choosing clothes and packing the materials I'd need for my events felt like a crushing weight, and I simply couldn't kick-start myself to begin. What eventually happened was a one-hour teary meltdown . . . 100 per cent originating from being bone tired.

So, take it from me: if motivation is currently failing you, start by getting some decent rest!

FIND SOMETHING WORTH GETTING MOTIVATED FOR

If you look up the definition of 'motivated', you'll learn that it is *'a reason or reasons for acting or behaving in a particular way'.*

We all know the bride who used her upcoming wedding as motivation to finally become the lean machine she'd wanted to be for years. Maybe you were that bride yourself! The vision of you looking drop-dead gorgeous in the wedding dress of your dreams, and walking up the aisle in front of all the people you love, feeling and looking incredible . . . that's a pretty magnetic vision.

Or you design a once-in-a-lifetime holiday to celebrate a milestone birthday, and for a year you diligently save $500 a month – as well as adding extra funds to the Dream Holiday bank account when you can. Every time you make a sacrifice – choosing a takeaway pizza over a fancy dinner, or wheeling out the dress you've worn 50 times already rather than splurging on something new – you visualise yourself sitting on that white, sandy beach with a cocktail in hand, and it feels worth it. Again, a magnetic vision.

Or you might decide to upskill by getting a new qualification, knowing that the professional development will put you in prime position for that promotion at work. On the nights where all you want to do is veg out with a wine and Netflix, or the mornings when you'd rather hit the snooze button than get an hour of study in before work, you see the increased responsibility, income and opportunity from that future promotion . . . and you hit the books. Another magnetic vision.

Here's my point, my dear. Settling on something that will truly ignite a spark within you will help infinitely with the motivation to get out there and make the shit you need and want to make happen, happen. That becomes your magnetic vision – that pulls you forward and towards the brighter version of you that you want for your life.

And remember my definition of purpose in the previous chapter? It's the guiding light that keeps you on course, even on the days when it feels impossible. Bring yourself back to that North Star to keep the motivational juices flowing.

OR YOU COULD JUST FORGET MOTIVATION ALTOGETHER

Someone I follow on Instagram recently gave me an excellent reframe (or alternative) to being motivated. Sarah Akwisombe, a UK-based entrepreneur and author, has enjoyed some awesome success – and some pretty hectic lows. After experiencing something of a 'life implosion' (as she termed it) in 2020, she embarked on a journey to get fit – seriously fit. She committed to doing a workout every morning, no matter what.

In an Instagram video, she explained that she didn't believe in motivation but rather that she believed in discipline. She freely admitted that some (or most!) mornings, the last thing she felt like doing was hitting the freezing-cold home gym in her garage in the dark, to push herself through her workout before her two daughters woke up. So if she was relying on motivation to get her out of bed and down to the gym, she was setting herself up for failure. Instead, she chose to believe in discipline – i.e. *'I said I'd do this, so I'm going to do it.'* Discipline, she said, doesn't allow room for internal bargaining.

You know what I'm talking about:

'I'll just let myself sleep in this morning and I'll do an extra workout tomorrow.'

'I've worked really hard this week already, so I can push that deadline I committed to back to next week.'

'I'll buy the dress/shoes/minibreak this month and make up the savings goal next month.'

We all do this – me included! What I love about Sarah's point is that it takes the brainwork out of it. You committed to doing whatever The Thing is, so you just do it; no bargaining, negotiating or back-and-forthing. You override that inner diva and just do what you said you'd do.

I get told I must be 'really motivated' all the time; however, I don't think I am. I'm just disciplined, and – in a weird way – discipline feels a lot more accessible to me than feeling the pressure to be constantly motivated. Being 100 per cent on fire is just not realistic, particularly when we throw into the mix curve balls like demanding clients, our partners' needs or children of all ages, never mind the day-to-day variability of our own energy.

But aiming for 100 per cent discipline? We can all do that.

THINK ABOUT THE EVIDENCE YOU'RE BUILDING FOR YOURSELF

Another epically helpful nugget that I come back to (and share with others) is one from US entrepreneur and author Rachel Hollis. She once shared a perspective that I had never thought of: that we as individuals are the only people in the whole world who bear witness to 100 per cent of what we do.

A big part of my work is one-on-one mentoring, and at the end of every mentoring session I help my mentee to set down a list of actions that they'll complete after our time together. I have no idea about, and no influence on, whether or not they choose to complete those actions (I have pretty much zero observational access to their lives outside of the time they spend with me).

Wade and I spend a lot of time together – often working together at home, eating most of our meals together and sleeping in the same bed. However, even with the hours of exposure he gets to me, he still doesn't see every single thing I do. Nor does Lexi, and nor does Wilder.

Regardless of how many people are in your household, or how people-focused your days are, you and you alone are the only person who bears witness to what you do each day. And Rachel's point? Knowing that fact, what evidence are you building for yourself as that witness to your own life? Are you breaking promises to yourself, or are you keeping them? Making realistic, attainable promises to ourselves – and keeping them – is the key to consistent motivation. That (as we know now) is really discipline dressed up in a different costume!

START WITH TINY

When a mentee or event participant tells me that 'they're just not a motivated person' and/or that 'they just don't follow through with things', I immediately ask them to share with me an example of this behaviour. Nine times out of ten, the reason they haven't 'stayed motivated' (in their words) is very simple: they were trying to do too much.

The amount of motivation required to achieve a goal directly correlates with how big that goal is. The bigger the goal, the more motivation that's required.

So, let's hack the system! If we set a tiny goal, we only need a little bit of motivation. The goal feels more achievable, and we are confident we can see it through consistently. Essentially, we create a positive feedback loop for ourselves.

I'll give you an example.

I was one of those people who for *years* said that I 'must' start meditating. I'd commit to meditating for 30 minutes every day, get into negotiations with myself (e.g. *'I won't meditate today or tomorrow, and I'll make up for it with an hour-long meditation at the weekend'*). It didn't work and – ultimately – there was no regular meditation practice happening.

So I switched it up, and started tiny. I made a promise to myself that I'd sit on the sofa for five minutes every morning and do some deep breathing. And so I did – consistently, for weeks.

Once I'd settled into that habit and proven to myself that I *could* be consistent, I increased the sofa time to ten minutes and started to learn about meditation practices. Now I can easily sit in meditation for 20 minutes at a time – in fact, the time usually flies by.

If motivation is a current or ongoing challenge for you, try the tiny approach and see how it can unlock motivation you didn't even know you had.

Please remember:

- *Everyone* struggles with motivation – even the most successful people who make everything look easy.
- High-achievers have developed an infrastructure for their lives that insures them against the inevitable days of Can't-Be-Fuckedness.

- Focus on discipline rather than motivation.
- Tiny steps will deliver more motivation than ambitious leaps forward.
- It *is* possible to keep your own promises to yourself.

Chapter 8

SETTING GOALS

I AM A BIG FAN OF SAYING 'I REALLY WISH THIS WAS TAUGHT IN schools!' about multiple life skills – you've already heard me say it about energy management. However, if I were forced to put only one thing – *one thing!* – on the school curriculum, it would be the skill of goal setting.

For many, many years my goal setting extended as far as making a handful of New Year's resolutions . . . and these pretty rapidly fizzled out by the end of January. In 2010 I set my first simple goals for the year, and my goal-setting process has developed from there – to the point that it's now a pretty comprehensive process, undertaken annually.

I've spent a lot of time teaching my community about goal setting – the importance of it, how to do it, and (of course) how to make those goals happen. In this chapter, I'm going to guide you through creating the ideal conditions for goal setting and take you through my process step-by-step. I'll share lots of examples as we go so that, by the end of this chapter, it will be crystal clear to you how to adopt the process into your own life.

I've also got every worksheet you need, ready to go – download your Step Into You Playbook for free from my website: lorrainemurphy.com.au/playbook.

Let's go . . .

THE POWER OF INTENTION

A tiny percentage of the population actually takes the time to set annual goals. So you can congratulate yourself on this point: simply by embarking on a process to set goals in your life, you're already in that VIP group!

I've realised that when we start to get intentional about our lives, that's when everything changes.

A few months ago, I did a declutter of my home office and came across the workbook for the very first personal development seminar I ever undertook, way back in 2010. Those two and a half days marked the first time I had ever taken time to reflect on my life: where I was and where I wanted to go. I set solid goals for the first time, and one of those goals was to one day own my own business.

The business took two years to come into being, but I know for sure that the seeds for it were planted back in that seminar.

And that's why I'm so excited to have you joining me for this chapter – I know that when you get clear, intentional and focused on your life plan, *everything* will shift for you.

MY CRITERIA FOR AN EFFECTIVE GOAL-SETTING SYSTEM

There are many different approaches that one could use to set goals – and a multitude of books, podcasts, online programs, seminars, templates and resources that one could access, spending anything from nothing at all to thousands of dollars for the privilege.

I've tried several different ways myself, borrowing the elements that worked and dumping those that didn't, and the process that I now work with – and teach – is the best one I've found. I'm fussy about how I do goal setting, and have four key criteria for it:

1. It needs to be simple

I have no space in my life for 20-page PDF documents. From my experience, they go in a drawer, I never look at them again, and therefore I get zero value from them. So many people (including me, once upon a time) overcomplicate this kind of work, and it's so unnecessary. Everything I do, when it comes to goal setting – and everything I'm taking you through in this chapter – is above all *simple*.

2. It needs to be fun

Goal setting shouldn't feel like a cross between a meeting with your accountant and root-canal therapy. It should be *fun*, it should be *exciting*. After all, you're getting to sit down and map out the life you dream of – how exciting is that!

3. It needs to start right now, as you are

You need to be able to start your goal setting right now, as your life stands in this exact moment. You shouldn't need to have lost weight/moved house/started a kid at school. You should be able to start it today.

4. It needs to unlock immediate momentum

Goal setting is totally irrelevant if we don't make shit happen as a result of it . . . and make it happen quickly. My process starts broad but by the end gets down to the nitty-gritty detail that will enable you to get started right away, therefore setting the pace for you to go and create this wonderful life you've mapped out for yourself.

SETTING THE CONDITIONS FOR GOAL SETTING

Something I believe a lot of people overlook when creating their goals is establishing the conditions for this special kind of thinking work. Just like in Chapter 6, in which I talked about opening up your heart space to access your purpose, we want to do some preparation before sitting down to set our goals.

1. Work in new surroundings

A big mistake that a lot of people make with their goal setting is that they sit in their usual daily surroundings to do this work. They might drop the kids at school, come home, make a cup of tea and sit down at the dining table (the same table they just had breakfast at, probably had dinner at the night before, and helped their kids with their homework on before that) to map out the life of their dreams.

These everyday environments – our dining table, our living room sofa, our offices, our bedrooms – are essentially wallpaper. We're in those spaces every day and don't really see/experience them anymore. Which is perfectly fine for everyday living, but not when we're trying to access a novel part of our brains to design our future lives.

It's really important when goal setting to remove ourselves from this daily wallpaper and find somewhere new, fresh and energising that will help us to generate fresh perspectives on what our lives could look like. This is why I will never do goal setting at home, and instead might take myself to a hotel for 24 hours, or if I'm planning with Wade, we'll go to a new beach, cafe or park to do the work. The new environment ushers in fresh ideas, fresh energy and fresh inspiration.

2. Get into your feminine energy

You'll be familiar with the idea of feminine energy from Chapter 4, and you'll know that feminine energy is creative energy. It can be all too easy to print out a batch of goal-setting templates and hit the ground running, filling them in as quickly as possible, but that's coming from a place of strong masculine energy. Goal setting isn't a fully linear, structured process – it actually requires a lot of creativity and imagination, especially in the earlier stages of the process. So it makes sense that – especially for women – we need to orientate ourselves in our feminine energy before we start on those goals.

I've shared lots of ideas on how you can do this in Chapter 4, however one way I 'prime' myself for goal setting is to move before I plan – I take a walk or a yoga class. I'll also try to get near to or in water. I had a super-powerful experience in water during one of my last 24-hour hotel planning stays.

I had taken myself away to a hotel in Bondi, which is only a 25-minute drive from home but felt like far enough for me to get those fresh surroundings I'm recommending to you. I was feeling quite lost with my business plans, given the COVID-19 pandemic had thrown a decent chunk of them off course (as it had for many people), and I was feeling the loss of momentum that came with that.

I was running the first bath I'd had in at least six months (maybe even a year!) and had treated myself to some beautiful bath salts. I hadn't been in the bath for longer than five minutes when an idea dropped right in for me: to start a Mastermind group. The idea was to assemble a group of my entrepreneur mentees, so they could learn from me, my team and each other. I had full clarity – who I'd invite, what I'd include, the team I'd need, what the price would be. As soon as I got out of the bath, I pulled out my sketch pad and coloured pens and mapped it out.

The week after my retreat, I shared the concept with my team, created an overview, presented it to those I wanted to invite . . . and two weeks later the Mastermind group was full. It also turned out to be the highest revenue stream in my business for the year. And it reminded me, once again, of how powerful our innate feminine creativity and intuition is when it comes to goal setting.

When we can get into that feminine energy, it's almost like we access a different level of ourselves, a different level of inspiration, creativity, clarity. If we take a masculine-energy approach, we're focused on the numbers, the details, the facts, and we cheat ourselves out of that higher level of thinking. As women, we can access a fast track to seeing our goals clearly. Prepare for your goal-setting session so that you're in an optimal state to fully access that beautiful, higher guidance as well.

3. Dress up for the occasion

I also suggest you dress up for your goal-setting session . . . even (or especially!) if you're doing it alone.

In the past, I've done my goal setting wearing a crappy hoodie that might have toothpaste on it, or the remnants of Lexi's breakfast. I've worn no make-up and had my hair (likely needing a wash) twisted up into a bun. I really didn't feel anywhere near fabulous. But what I've been doing for the last couple of years is getting dressed up for the occasion – wearing something that makes me feel great and making an effort with my hair and make-up. The difference has been remarkable!

The reason is that I feel like I'm dressing up for my Future Self – and, when I'm feeling and looking good, my vibe is high. And *that's* the space that I want to be designing my Dream Lifestyle from.

4. Create some little treats for yourself

I need to be really clear here: I am NOT saying you need to drop hundreds or thousands of dollars on indulgent stuff in order to set effective goals. I am, however, saying that you want to give yourself treats that will, first of all, greatly enhance your own pleasure and enjoyment while you set your goals and, secondly, remind you that you're *worthy* of nice things.

When I do my planning, I allow myself to have some nice food. I enjoy a new essential oil blend. I get out the bath salts. I treat myself to a tea that might be a couple of dollars more per pack than I'd ordinarily spend on tea for our household. I let myself light the nice candle. I do this as I want to believe that I'm worthy of things . . . and worthy of my dream life.

5. Plan in the time to plan

If I got my hands on your calendar, I'd recommend a half to a full day of planning time. That's to give yourself time to move through the entire process with space and breaks. And I would also – ideally – ask you to do this planning in one block so that you can flow with the process as I've designed it.

That said, something is better than nothing. I know it's not going to be possible for everyone to devote a full day or even a half-day to the task. There are careers, families and social lives to work around. So if you need to, break the process down into chunks and be very, very intentional about making each of those opportunities happen.

Book the time in your diary upfront. Remember, you're worth this time. You're worth the life that you dream of!

MY GOAL-SETTING PROCESS

Here's an overview of the process we're about to work through together.

First, we'll define your Dream Lifestyle. From there we'll create your Five-Year Vision. And we'll break that down to a One-Year Vision. Next, we'll set a clear list of goals. After that we'll create your 90-Day Plan. And, lastly, we'll look at the person you need to be.

1. Define your Dream Lifestyle

Recently, when I was undertaking a 24-hour planning block, I sat down to begin what was then my first goal-setting step – mapping my Five-Year Vision – and discovered that it just wasn't coming. I didn't have the clarity I usually did about how I wanted my life to look in five years' time. Trying to define the business, revenue and home I wanted . . . I just couldn't *see* it.

So I backed up a step and focused on what I wanted my Dream Lifestyle to look like. I figured that if I could clearly articulate the lifestyle I wanted to have, the other components would become clear from there.

And it worked! Taking the focus off the 'how' and instead focusing on the 'what' of the life I wanted to be working towards gave me the jumping-off point to flow through the rest of the process. It also made goals more real and tangible, rather than just pulling numbers out of thin air. These days I always start with this step.

So let's do it. The Dream Lifestyle worksheet is part of your Step Into You Playbook that you can download from lorrainemurphy. com.au/playbook.

Think about how your lifestyle would look if you were living *the absolute dream* – and get that down on your worksheet. This doesn't need to be exhaustive; two or three points per section is perfect.

This is what I call a blue-sky exercise. It doesn't require you to get too weighed down in details – the aim of the rest of the planning process is to do that.

Most of the categories are self-explanatory, but I wanted to linger for a moment on the Nice Things section. These are the items or experiences that make you feel, well, *nice*. It may seem superficial, but I believe these things are important for the same reasons that I dress up or treat myself when I do my goal setting: they make me feel good and affirm that I'm worthy of dreaming of nice things. It's that simple.

To give you some examples, the nice things in my own Dream Lifestyle are:

- a gorgeous wardrobe and, even though I don't actually shop very much, the ability to walk into any shop and buy anything I'd like to have
- a weekly blow-dry – a standing appointment with my hairdresser so my hair looks amazing all the time
- a monthly night away in a hotel on my own, to have space and time to myself with no agenda and no-one else to look after

Another section I want to spell out a little is Giving Back. This is going to be unique to everyone. For some it's already built into their work (for example, they might work for a charity), for some it'll be donating their time to a cause they're passionate about, and for some it might mean making ongoing financial contributions to a cause or causes that matter to them. For me, it's donating a portion of ticket sales from certain events I run to a charity whose work I really love.

IMPORTANT NOTE

You don't need to place a specific timeframe on achieving your Dream Lifestyle – whether what you create is achievable in 12 months or 12 years is irrelevant. The important thing is that it gives you some kind of a handle on how you want to be living your life, and gets your creative juices flowing for the rest of the process.

PONDER THIS

Often, some of the things we identify for our Dream Lifestyle are immediately achievable. One mentee of mine, Amanda, worked alongside me to do this exercise and identified that she'd like to do yoga and meditate six days a week. I said to her: 'You know you could just do that right now?'

Ask yourself, when you've completed this activity, what elements of your Dream Lifestyle could be addressed or achieved *right now*. Circle those things. It might require some budgeting, some rejigging of priorities and some planning – but it could well be possible straightaway . . . which is pretty cool!

2. Create your Five-Year Vision

Way back in 2012 I was a couple of months into my first business, and feeling uncertain as to how to further build it, when I came across an excellent business book, *Mastering the Rockefeller Habits* by Verne Harnish. I still consider it the best business book I've ever read, but at the time, the biggest help I drew from it was the concept of planning with just three horizons in mind:

1. five years
2. one year
3. the next 90 days

I put the concept into action for my business planning, and everything started to fall into place from then on.

You can find my Five-Year Vision worksheet in your Step Into You Playbook. This is the worksheet I've used myself for years, and it's the one that Wade and I work through when we plan our annual goals every January.

IMPORTANT NOTE

We're not into specific goal setting yet! The purpose of the Five-Year Vision is to paint the picture of the life you wish to have, and ensure that the various bases are covered via the 12 categories below.

First off, at the top of the page write what the date will be in five years' time. This is the date by which your vision will be happening for you.

You'll see that there are 12 categories:

1. family
2. home
3. business/career
4. filling your tank
5. finance

6. travel
7. significant other
8. giving back
9. friends/community
10. development
11. health
12. other

To make this extra-easy for you to complete, I've also recorded a visualisation exercise that will help you to bring this Five-Year Vision to life. You can download the audio track at lorrainemurphy. com.au/playbook.

Have the worksheet from your Step Into You Playbook ready to go, then listen to the visualisation exercise. Once you're finished, treat the worksheet as a home for a brain dump of what dropped in for you during the visualisation. Specific goals aren't important at this point – we're simply trying to capture the picture of your life that you saw in your mind's eye at this future date in five years' time.

3. Now distil your One-Year Vision

Now that you've got some clarity on where you want to be in five years' time, you're ready to break that down to what you want life to look like in 12 months' time. Grab the One-Year Vision worksheet from the playbook. You'll see that this is the very same format as the Five-Year Vision worksheet – remember, we're keeping this *simple*!

Just like we did last time, write down the future date (aka exactly one year from today) and identify the different parts of the picture of your life using the 12 categories. Again, we're not honing in on super-specific goals, we're just painting the picture.

4. Set your goals

Now that we've got a reasonably solid picture of your Five-Year and One-Year Visions, it's time to break them down into clear goals. This is where we get specific: what *exactly* are you going to do over the next 12 months in order to land you neatly on the doorstep of your One-Year Vision?

This is the easy bit, my friend, as you've already done the big thinking and visualising. Go to my Goal Setting worksheet from the playbook at lorrainemurphy.com.au/playbook and start listing those special goals of yours. You'll see that the categories flow on exactly from the categories in the vision worksheets, so it should be quite straightforward for you to complete this next step.

I've allowed space here for three goals per category, but you might have fewer than that, or more. For me, for example, I'll generally have two or three development goals, but 10 or 12 business goals.

5. Create your 90-Day Plan

This is when the rubber hits the road! Creating a 90-Day Plan was a game changer when I adopted Verne Harnish's approach all those years ago. Since then, for almost ten years now, I've made a quarterly plan. I can't wait to share it with you . . .

Ninety days is an ideal window of time as a) it gives us enough time to complete a decent-sized goal or project, and b) it's not *so much time* that we can succumb to procrastination or inertia.

Back when I was employed, I would have my annual review and in it set a 12-month development plan with my manager. I'd be full of motivation for about a month, then gradually the plan would be forgotten . . . and ultimately relegated to my bottom drawer, only to be remembered again in a panic a month out from my next annual review.

This is why I think the 90-Day Plan is brilliant – it gives us momentum, but also enough time to get shit done. First off, grab the template from my Step Into You Playbook and I'll step you through it.

1. You'll see that the plan is structured around five core 'rocks'. Rocks are your big projects or themes for the quarter ahead. In the worksheet I've given you an example of starting an email newsletter, however you could just as easily make one of your rocks 'declutter the house'. Identify what your five rocks will be for the next 90 days.

2. Next you'll be asked to articulate your intention for that particular rock. For the email newsletter example, I've said it's 'to share my message with our audience and generate sales leads'. For the house-decluttering rock, it might be 'to have an airy, bright and clear sanctuary at home'.

3. From there, you'll break down *exactly* what you'll do within that rock – step by step. I like to see this as my 'recipe' for making that rock happen!

4. And then you'll specify how you'll know it's done – whether that's a financial target or a number of rooms decluttered. If I

arrived on your doorstep at the end of these 90 days, how would I know it was done?

5. Lastly, you'll identify your reward. This is the fun bit! Here you write what special thing you'll get as a result of making all of this happen. It's really important we do this, as it provides the carrot to keep on keeping on, especially on those days when it's the very last thing we feel like doing. Plus, once we earn our reward it creates a positive feedback loop for us to do the same next quarter.

IMPORTANT NOTE

Before we move to the last step of my goal-setting process, I need to share what one of my business coaches, Ronan Powell, told me that totally reframed goal setting for me. He explained that people get stuck on what they'll 'have' as a result of their goal setting, and fast-track straight to the 'have' part of their goals:

> *'I want to have the mortgage paid off.'*
> *'I want to have my business making $1 million a year.'*
> *'I want to have four amazing holidays.'*
> *'I want to have the partner of my dreams.'*

It's all have, have, have. And for some reason, often having these things or people or experiences eludes us. Ronan said what we should be considering as well is the 'do' part of our goals – i.e: what are we actually *doing* so that we can *have* these elements in our lives?

So if we want to *have* the mortgage paid off, we need to *do* some intentional and consistent saving so that we can put that extra cash against the mortgage. If we want to *have* our business making $1 million a year, we need to *do* the hard yards in marketing, sales and scaling up our team.

But the most critical aspect of all, as Ronan explained, is the person we are *being* day to day – that person who is doing what needs to be done in order to have the things they want to have. The best way to get what we want to have is to *be the person who can have it and deserve it.*

So in the mortgage example, that person who is on a mission to pay off their mortgage will need to *be* disciplined and consistent. The person building a million-dollar business will need to *be* courageous and strategic.

Consider the 'do' and 'be' aspects of your goals and these will help lead you to the 'have'.

6. Who do you need to be in order to achieve your goals?

I would argue that, of all the planning I do as part of this goal-setting process, this question is the most potent. It makes me realise that in order to make all these amazing things happen, I'm going to have to carry myself in a certain way, day to day. And as I'm ambitious, many of my goals are goals I haven't previously achieved – so in some ways I'll need to actually *be* a different person than the person I currently am.

Grab the worksheet titled The Person I Need To Be from your Step Into You Playbook at lorrainemurphy.com.au/playbook. Now, ask yourself the question: *What person do I need to be in order to make all of this happen?*

Do you need to be focused, disciplined, brave, cautious, optimistic, hardworking, educated, resourceful, collaborative, proactive, considered, organised, detail-orientated, a blue-sky thinker?

Identify the kind of person you need to be (I've given you six sections on the worksheet), then clearly state three ways you can demonstrate that in your life.

For example, one of the characteristics I need to be in order to achieve my goals is *disciplined*. And to do this, I:

- do what I say I'll do
- have a clear structure for my quarters, months, weeks and days
- say no to what's not on the plan

SOME POINTS TO KEEP IN MIND

There you have it, my friend – my complete goal-setting process! I just have a few more points I want to share with you before we move onto the next step of this journey . . .

Timings can be hard to predict

Sometimes it's difficult to estimate just how long it will take to make something happen, but do not let this lack of clarity become a story that stops you from getting started.

The important thing is that we set some kind of timeline – and that we get moving on it. With time and practice, we then become more adept at knowing how long certain goals will likely take to reach. So if you're not sure if something belongs in the Five-Year

Vision or the One-Year Vision, go with your gut and put it where that leads you.

Our brains will access these visions differently

I've noticed that, for some people, the Five-Year Vision flows effortlessly, whereas the One-Year Vision finds them struggling. And for others, the difficulty lies in wrapping their heads around what their life might be like in five years' time, yet their One-Year Vision is super-clear. You might find both are easy to conjure up, or that both are equally difficult.

Cut yourself some slack. Our brains are all wired differently!

Some clarity is better than full clarity

There is no expectation that you nail this entire process from beginning to end, first time around. Goal setting isn't necessarily a linear process, where we tick the relevant boxes and – voila! – it's all wrapped up with a pretty bow. You'll have some areas that are crystal clear and some areas that are seriously blurry. The out-of-focus areas might arise from not having enough information yet, or from being dependent on other people or events falling into place. That's totally fine!

I often use the analogy of a GPS system in these instances. Let's say I'm going to visit my friend Sarah in the suburb of Marrickville – but I can't for the life of me remember her street address. If I tap 'Marrickville' into Google Maps, it's going to land me a hell of a lot closer to Sarah's house than if I gave up and just stayed at home.

So get as close as you can with your Five-Year and One-Year Visions, and the blurry areas will come into focus in their own time.

Allow for flexibility

I set my goals at the start of 2020, and then COVID-19 hit. That resulted in my goals needing to change. The thing is, life does tend to happen: redundancies, new babies, interstate or overseas moves, new relationships, or relationships breaking down . . . or simply a feeling that a goal isn't for you anymore.

Please don't go into a goal-setting exercise believing that everything needs to be carved in stone, tattooed on your forehead and/ or published on the front page of a national newspaper! Build in some flex for yourself and give yourself a hall pass from the rigid thinking that can so easily spell the end of a dream. Remember that there is more than just one route to your destination, and it's vitally important that we enjoy the journey.

There's no 'right way' of doing all of this

In this chapter I'm sharing with you a process that I've created, fiddled with, practised and fiddled with again, refining it over a period of almost ten years. Even though this process works for me and the hundreds of mentees I've guided through it, I still invite you to tweak it to work for you and your unique situation. So, add or subtract sections from the worksheets, do them in the reverse order to what I've suggested, incorporate some ideas from other teachers – just do you.

Please remember: ~~~~~~

- When we get intentional about our lives, *everything* changes.
- Goal setting shouldn't be laborious, boring or complicated.
- Creating the conditions for goal setting helps to infuse clarity and high vibes into the process.
- Defining your unique Dream Lifestyle can help crystallise goals that might be vague otherwise.
- The three goal-setting horizons we work to are: five years, one year and 90 days.
- Focusing on the person we want to *be*, rather than what we want to *have*, is a much more aligned way of thinking.

Part 4

Make it happen

Let's get serious momentum and transformation underway – it's time to translate your goals and ideas into real-life, achievable actions . . .

Chapter 9

THE KEY TO EFFECTIVE (AND SUSTAINED) CHANGE

LET'S HAVE A CHECK-IN, SHALL WE? SO FAR IN OUR STEP INTO YOU adventure together we have:

- cleared any negative beliefs that may have been holding you back
- taken stock of where your life is at
- explored some ideas around how you can generate – and maintain – more energy
- tuned into your purpose
- made some tweaks to getting you more motivated
- created a compelling vision and set of goals for you and the life you dream of living

I'm so proud of you!

So what's next?

Change is not easy. And it's certainly not easy to consistently show up to make changes day by day, week by week and month by month. If you've ever started a radical new exercise or nutrition plan, you'll be familiar with the buzz you feel those first two or three days. The novelty factor is high, motivation is off the charts, and you're filled with excitement about the 'new you' that's emerging.

By day three, or maybe day four if you're doing super-well, the novelty starts to wear off. The lifestyle changes you were undertaking start to feel a lot more laborious than they did a couple of days ago. You miss your old patterns: the dark chocolate you looked forward to every afternoon, or hitting the snooze button instead of getting up for an early-morning work-out. An opportunity to deviate from the new regimen arrives in the form of a social invitation, or you tell yourself you deserve a pick-me-up (you know, 'I've had a shitty day so I deserve X, Y, Z').

Gradually the dazzling appeal of the New You starts to fade, until a week or two later you're beating yourself up about your lack of commitment/motivation/discipline and general inability to be a great human.

Oh, and then your old friend Comparisonitis kicks in to really drive the neggy vibes home for you. You look at friends, colleagues or Instagram fitspo models who – somehow – seem to have been gifted with a gene that enables them to make positive changes in their lives. You must have been in the bathroom when your Creator was handing those genes out.

In this chapter we're going to focus on setting you up for success in making positive changes in your life . . . and sustaining them over the long haul.

HOW OVERCOMING RESISTANCE IS KEY IN MAKING CHANGES

I first learnt about the concept of 'resistance' from Steven Pressfield, in his book *Do the Work*. It's primarily about the creative process, and overcoming our own internal resistance to move ourselves through what can be a self-doubting and fear-filled experience.

However, the principles he shares apply to every area of our lives – especially when it comes to making positive changes in them.

So, what is resistance, according to Pressfield?

Resistance is the internal pull away from what we know is good for us. That could be eating better, updating our résumé, asking for the promotion, tackling a relationship issue head-on, starting that side hustle . . . Anything that requires us to step out of our safe and secure comfort zone and stretch is guaranteed to be served with a hefty side of resistance.

When I happened upon this concept, it created a mindset revolution for me! Firstly as, for the first time, I understood *why* I often felt so blocked when it came to doing new or scary things; secondly as I understood that it was *perfectly normal*. And just like when we're experiencing some kind of physical symptom, once we have our medical diagnosis we can actually *do* something about it.

Resistance shows up in many insidious ways in our lives, including (but not limited to):

- procrastination
- self-sabotage
- negative self-talk
- over-reliance on the opinions of others
- inertia
- perfectionism (a big one)

Funnily enough, this list also directly equates to the most common mindset blocks I help my mentees with. Could resistance actually be the root cause of most of the apparent mindset challenges we think we have? And what can we do about it?

Here are some answers . . .

1. Accept it

Fighting resistance is like flinging petrol on a blazing fire – it just makes it burn even harder. So step one in dealing with resistance is to acknowledge that that's what's happening. Just like the sun rising in the sky, like trees shedding their leaves in autumn, resistance is a part of life.

This book started its life as a proposal. Then my publisher asked me to write a couple of sample chapters. I scheduled a morning to get started on it, and it was as if every single resistance monster was rearing its ugly and maddening head.

I faffed around on every social media channel, news site and inbox I had access to. *(Procrastination.)*

I told myself my book idea was total and utter shite and no-one would ever want to read it. *(Negative self-talk.)*

I sat there doing *absolutely nothing* for at least 20 minutes. *(Inertia.)*

When I actually finished writing, I fiddled and re-fiddled with individual words and punctuation. *(Perfectionism.)*

It was *exhausting*!

And then I finally realised what this all was: I was experiencing RESISTANCE.

And guess what? When I put a name to it, the resistance instantly dropped away.

2. Just begin

Easier said than done, I know! But remember that most of the pain of resistance comes from not acknowledging it. Once you've done that, it *does* get easier.

Then you've got to get started – otherwise resistance wins.

To draw again on the example of me writing this book, those first few black letters that I typed into a Word document were agonising – they came in faltering, mechanical spurts. And then they started to come a little easier, and then easier again, and – finally – I was in full flow. After two hours I had 4,000 words written.

My all-time favourite quote is this one – Irish professor John Anster's interpretation of a line from Goethe's play *Faust*:

> *'Whatever you can do or dream you can, begin it. Boldness has genius, power and magic in it.'*

I have experienced the truth of this sentiment many times over.

Most people I meet have a business idea in them somewhere, but the vast majority of them won't ever start it. Maybe it's because they don't believe their idea will work, that someone else is already doing it, that they wouldn't make enough money, that they'll need to work too hard, that they'd never survive the embarrassment if it failed . . . or maybe all of the above.

When I started my first business in 2012, I had all of these thoughts . . . and probably a few more. But the thought of '*If not now, then when?*' spurred me on to map out my idea, talk to a few people about it, work out some very rough numbers, do some research . . . and finally take the leap of resigning from my job and starting it.

There is no reason that that business should have succeeded. I was a first-time entrepreneur. My idea had never been done before in Australia (and hardly done around the world). I had no sales experience. I had no finance experience. I didn't have a strong network. I had no financial backers. I was at least a year ahead of the influencer-marketing curve.

However, the business found its feet, and then went on to be a huge success.

Yes, I worked hard. But if you were to ask me the true reason for the success of that business, I would have to answer you honestly: *I started it.*

3. And then keep going

Even if you think your work-out was crap, even if you *know* the résumé you're working on is terrible, even if you don't think you'll ever get to the bottom of the clutter in the spare room, even if you think you'll never be able to prep your meals for the week . . . *just keep going.*

And at every step of the way, at every shitty thought you have about your own ability and commitment, remember that this is *exactly* what resistance wants you to do – and you're bigger than resistance.

My second book, *Get Remarkably Organised*, has been my most successful to date – successful in terms of the number of books sold, but also in terms of the positive impact it's had on thousands of readers. Readers tell me they've read it five times, that it's 'their Bible', and they invest even more of their time and money in me and my business as a result of reading the book.

And yet it was a *struggle* to write. Not because I didn't know my stuff when it came to organisation (it's my jam), but because I questioned incessantly the value of what I was writing.

Imagine if I'd stopped midway through and called my publisher to back out of the deal? That book wouldn't have helped the people it did, I would have cheated myself out of deep fulfilment and I'd have deprived my business of opportunities.

Even if – *especially if* – you think what you're doing has no value, keep on going. That is effective self-leadership at its very finest.

THE CHALLENGES OF OVERCOMING RESISTANCE

Now that you have a handle on the beast that resistance can be, I need to share two vitally important points towards helping you tame it.

Shipping it

In his book *Do the Work*, Steven Pressfield drives home the importance of 'shipping it'.

'Shipping it' means completing the piece of work – whether it's
the last week of an eight-week fitness program or sending your business plan to a potential investor. Earlier in this chapter I described
beginning as often the most difficult part of resistance . . . however,
finishing it can be *the* most difficult. That's because that final
flourish is resistance's last opportunity to stop us in our tracks, to
hold us back from that positive step or change. At the very point
that we're about to finish, resistance peaks.

Even if I've been working on a business proposal for weeks,
hitting 'send' on it to a potential client is crazy-hard. Or publishing
a podcast episode that's particularly close to my heart. But once our
idea/work/commitment is out there, completed in the real world,
resistance no longer has any power over us . . . and we get to feel
that deep contentment and 'fuck yeah!' that we finished something.

The bigger the deal, the higher the resistance

This is really, really important to note. Resistance doesn't come
as a one-size-fits-all poncho. The scale of the resistance we have
to deal with is in direct proportion to how important that goal or
change is to us.

I would like to think that I've mastered overcoming procrastination – indeed, it's been a key life skill in helping me build the
businesses I've built, completed the creative projects I've completed
and generally gotten shit done day to day.

However, starting this book rose all my procrastination ghosts up from the dead! And – now that I understand resistance – the reason is clear.

This book is a big deal for me. It packages up all the biggest lessons I've learned from thousands of hours of mentoring, running retreats and events, hosting webinars, running online programs and trying, testing, learning and often failing at applying my ideas in my own life.

I've gotten to help thousands of women through my work: over countless conversations, Instagram DMs and emails. And I want to help thousands more with this book.

As I was starting to write, I was paralysed: because I know how important this book is to me, and how important it can be to other women.

The result? Resistance was at an all-time high and I needed to dig even deeper than usual to overcome it.

So if you've battled resistance, gotten started, and plugged away like a diligent workhorse on the decidedly unsexy work of showing up every day for yourself, and you're shocked that resistance is *still* hanging in there attempting to make your life miserable, do not be surprised. It's just a part of the process.

Really understanding and integrating a plan of attack against resistance will give you an immeasurable edge on sustaining true transformational change that this book you're reading can create in your life. It's been probably my biggest lesson in creating new things and making growth happen for myself, and I'm thrilled I can pass it on to you as part of this chapter.

Please remember: ~~~~~~~~~~~~~~~~

- It's not easy to consistently show up to make a new goal a reality.
- Understanding the concept of resistance is the key to sustained change.
- Resistance manifests in our lives in many forms, including procrastination, self-sabotage, negative self-talk, overdependence on the opinions of others, inertia and perfectionism.
- Practising acceptance is step one in dealing with resistance.
- Beginning is the second hardest stage in battling resistance.
- Persisting with a goal is self-leadership at its very finest.
- Resistance peaks right before we finish a project, and can be harder to overcome the bigger the project is.

Chapter 10

STAYING ON TRACK

NOW, I'VE HAD THE PRIVILEGE OF GETTING THE INSIDE SCOOP OF many women's goals, aspirations, wins and challenges over the years, and I've seen women smash their goals out of the park . . . and fall off track with them.

I spent some time analysing *why* exactly those who fall off track do so, and I came up with five main reasons:

1. self-doubt – questioning their ability, experience and ambition
2. overcommitting – taking on too much
3. forgetting their 'why' – losing touch with the reason they're attempting the goal in the first place
4. curve balls – holidays, illnesses, hectic work periods
5. breaking promises to themselves – not doing what they said they'd do

If you're reading this thinking, *'tick, tick, tick,'* do not fear; I come bearing tools! Let's work through each of these reasons and what the antidotes are . . .

1. SELF-DOUBT

Self-doubt is a lack of confidence in one's own abilities. It's questioning our own capacity, our own passion, our own appropriateness – and a subset of self-doubt is most definitely imposter syndrome!

There are two tactics that we can use to combat self-doubt's ability to take us off track:

1. manage our negative self-talk
2. create an affirmation practice

Manage negative self-talk

Every one of us has the capacity to speak negatively to ourselves, and it's a tricky thing to navigate.

When I'm working with a mentee one on one, I am constantly on the lookout for clues on their self-talk. When I notice a negative or self-limiting pattern, I call it out to them. It constantly amazes me how shocked they are when I point out a negative spin to them!

Here are three self-talk patterns to nix immediately if you notice them:

NEGATIVE SELF-TALK PATTERN 1: *'I NEED TO . . .'*

This one might seem innocuous but I have a particular aversion to it, for one simple reason: it heaps pressure on us. I would bet that the average person has at least ten 'I need to' thoughts bouncing around in their brain on any one day.

'I need to put some laundry on.'
'I need to get back to X on Y.'
'I need to get to bed earlier.'
'I need to work harder.'
'I need to be more present.'

'I need to' is very often accompanied by any combo of *'Why haven't I done that already?'*, *'What's wrong with me?'*, *'Why am I always so lazy/tired/afraid/undisciplined?'* etc.

Now I know that we all *need* to get things done – to work, live, pay taxes, live in reasonably tidy homes. But what if we replace 'need' with 'want', and explain to ourselves the 'why' of wanting to do a thing? It changes the whole energy of our self-talk!

'I need to clean this house' is a very different statement from *'I want to clean the house [so it's fresh for the week ahead].'*

'I need to get this report done' is quite different from *'I want to get this done [so I can get on to more interesting tasks].'*

Replacing the *'need'* structure with *'want and why'* pops a pin in the pressure bubble we build for ourselves, and also gives us more of an understanding of why we want to get something done . . . and that's infinitely more motivating!

NEGATIVE SELF-TALK PATTERN 2: 'I AM SO STUPID/LAZY/MEAN/ DISORGANISED'

A really handy lens to use to establish if our self-talk is healthy is to ask ourselves: *'Would I speak to my best friend/child/most important client in this way?'* If the answer is no, then some urgent and consistent self-correction is required.

I (most of the time) speak with love, faith and encouragement to Lexi, as does Wade. She gets told at least a dozen times a day how amazing she is, how much we love her, and how perfect she is. And we mean it!

If I compare how I speak to her with how I sometimes speak to myself, the difference is radical. I'll catch myself, after making a mistake, berating myself for my lack of planning or sheer stupidity.

Thankfully I usually spot my negative self-talk and replace it with a more positive spin.

Remember that your internal conversation is just that: a conversation. It's NOT based on facts.

NEGATIVE SELF-TALK PATTERN 3: *'YOU WILL NEVER, EVER [INSERT LIFE ACHIEVEMENT OF CHOICE HERE]'*

Finish university, find a great partner, write a book, have enough money, get the dream job, start the business, have a family, have enough time, get enough sleep, have enough sex, go on that holiday . . .

Our negative self-talk LOVES to tell us all the things we'll never do! Know this for what it is: resistance holding us back. *That's it.*

Remember that what we think on a regular basis becomes our reality. So if we tell ourselves we'll never meet a great partner, guess what happens? If we tell ourselves our business will always struggle, guess what happens? If we tell ourselves we'll never catch up on sleep, guess what happens?

If someone spends their mental downtime imagining how wonderful it would be to build a dream house, do you think they're more likely to succeed in having that house than someone who tells themselves over and over that they'll be stuck in their too-small semi for the rest of their lives? I'll leave that one to you.

Don't put unnecessary obstacles in your path. Tell yourself, 50 times a day if you need to, that your life achievement IS possible. What have you got to lose?

Create an affirmation practice

Affirmations are very closely linked to negative self-talk. They are positive, uplifting statements that fill the vacuum created by ripping out all that crappy stuff we can say to ourselves.

I've had an affirmation practice for many years. Here's why:

- **They keep me on track.** Do you remember when you went tenpin bowling as a kid and sometimes they'd put those big cushions along the lane, so no matter how terrible your throw was, you'd still manage to hit at least one pin? That's how I see affirmations.
- **They act as 'pattern interrupters'.** The idea of a *pattern interrupt* comes from neuro-linguistic programming (NLP), and it essentially means that if we're engaged in a negative activity – for example, berating ourselves with negative self-talk – we use something powerful to stop us in our tracks and switch to a much more positive mindset. If I catch myself in a downward mental spiral of worry/shame/fear, I'll whip out one of my affirmations and say that to myself, to break the pattern.

- **They anchor me in times of stress, self-doubt or uncertainty.**
  If I float too far away from where I want to be, my daily affirmation practice gently brings me back there.

HOW TO DO AN AFFIRMATION PRACTICE

Ideally, you want to repeat your own set of affirmations twice a day. For me, that's when I'm getting ready for the day, and last thing before I go to bed at night. Say them out loud, and with emotion and emphasis. You can even do them in the mirror; there's something powerful about actively making eye contact with yourself as you say your affirmations. (And if you're learning new affirmations, a mirror serves as a useful space to write them down with a whiteboard marker!)

Use specific affirmations at any point that you need them. For example, for me, during my pregnancies, I repeated my affirmations multiple times a day as a balm for my anxious soul.

WHAT AFFIRMATIONS TO SAY

So you're probably wondering right now, 'This is all great Lorraine, but what affirmations do I actually *say?!*' Don't worry, I have got you covered! I've brought together 201 of the most powerful affirmations that I've encountered just for you. You can find them in your Step Into You Playbook that you can download from my website at lorrainemurphy.com.au/playbook.

You'll see that the affirmations are organised into particular sections: Faith, Love, Happiness, etc. I suggest you read through the affirmations and make a note of the ones that resonate with you, or that you feel an instinctive pull to.

Choose 8–10 affirmations that you want to work with for now – think of it like your unique suite of affirmations! Remember that you can switch up your affirmations at any point, this practice is totally yours for the creating.

2. OVERCOMMITTING

Overcommitting can include taking on too big of a goal, too great a chunk of a goal, having too many competing commitments, or working to an unrealistic timeline to achieve a goal.

Overcommitment is a major killer of goals. The reason? It just gets too bloody hard and we give up! You might be wanting to make some major changes in your life (maybe losing a significant amount of weight, or exiting an unhealthy relationship), or you're taking on a goal that scares the bejesus out of you (say, quitting a corporate job to start your own business, or making a long-distance move).

Remember that these changes or goals won't just happen – they're stretching you into a new version of you, and with that comes the need for a considered, strategic approach. We don't go from zero to hero overnight!

So how can we make these changes or goals happen, in a way that won't have us running scared for the hills? Two tools we'll explore here are:

1. micro-horizons
2. habit layering

Micro-horizons

In his book *Built to Last*, Jim Collins coined the term BHAG, or Big Hairy Audacious Goal. Using micro-horizons is for you if you've got a BHAG in mind, but the sheer scale of it has you feeling paralysed. The idea is super-simple: rather than seeing your objective as the one and only horizon, break it down into a series of smaller horizons.

Let me explain . . .

In 2018 we attempted a tree-change move to the Gold Coast in Queensland. We bought a house and moved in, but after three months I was losing my mind with loneliness and it was decided we'd move back to Sydney. We felt totally overwhelmed by the idea of executing the move, just four months after we'd packed up our whole lives and schlepped it north. We couldn't fathom doing it all over again. So we broke it down into four micro-horizons:

1. find a tenant for our Queensland house
2. find a home in Sydney
3. plan and book the move to Sydney
4. set up our new life in Sydney

I cannot tell you how much relief this exercise brought to our stress levels! It gave us a clear focus for a few weeks at a time, and – this is critical – we didn't allow ourselves to jump ahead to future horizons until the one we were currently focusing on was completed. That meant that when I started to worry about getting Lexi into a day care in Sydney, I snapped myself back to the fact that, right now, the focus was on finding a removalist to get our stuff down south again.

Micro-horizons are an excellent way to approach intimidating goals or tasks. And remember, you can break those goals or tasks down into as many micro-horizons as you want to. If having 37 micro-horizons helps you sleep at night, go for gold!

Habit layering

This tool is for you if you're on a mission to implement consistent changes in your life – for example, getting more exercise, having a morning routine, making time for a creative endeavour . . . you get the idea.

Many people simply bite off more than they can chew when they're making these changes in their lives. We've all known – and been! – that person who commits to a new exercise regimen and staggers around the house or office the day after their first work-out, their muscles in agony. But they (we!) are also thrilled, as it shows the exercise is working. By the time Day 3 rolls around, the novelty is starting to wear off, and by Day 7 it's nowhere to be found. And before they/we know it, we've stopped going to the gym or answering our running buddy's calls.

The problem here is that the gap between where the person was (i.e. not very fit at all) and where they wanted to be (i.e. a total machine) was too big, and flinging themselves headlong into a vigorous training program was pre-emptive for them.

So what do we do? Again, we break it down.

Rather than committing to five exercise classes a week, instead we commit to two – and we make them happen. Once two classes feels like it's working well and isn't a huge stretch, we add on another class, then another, then another.

Over a period of weeks (or more likely, months) we find we're able to accommodate the five classes a week . . . and we're keeping them up.

I took this approach to putting a morning routine in place. I went from someone who had zero morning routine to someone who consistently spent an hour each morning setting herself up for the day. But I didn't do it in one fell swoop (that failed). Instead I layered the habits gradually.

First of all, I got up ten minutes earlier.

Then I started meditating for five minutes.

Then the meditation stretched to ten minutes. And then 15 minutes.

Then I started to do some visualisation.

Then I added a morning lemon drink.

My point here is that the morning routine took *months* to create. I stretched my own discipline and commitment as the morning routine grew.

So if there's a habit that you want to bring into your life, break it down into a series of smaller habits. That approach spells sure success!

3. FORGETTING OUR WHY

This pitfall is a common one: we're progressing with a goal and it starts to feel a bit lacklustre, and like a lot more *effort* than it was previously. We question why we're even doing it in the first place – we forget our why.

In Chapter 6 we talked about purpose being the North Star of our lives. Ideally we have one primary purpose (mine, as I've said, is to help women rise even higher in their lives), however individual goals will likely have an inbuilt 'purpose/why' to them too.

For example:

The goal: Lose 10 kg
The why: To have more energy and wear clothes I love again

The goal: Save $800 per month
The why: To give myself financial opportunities in future

The goal: To have 5000 Instagram followers
The why: To make my side hustle a viable business

So how do we stay connected with the 'whys' of our goals? Two ways:

1. We create a motivating, magnetic vision board.
2. We track our progress.

The power of a vision board

A vision board is, very simply, a visual representation of the life we wish to be leading. Just like the Dream Lifestyle exercise, it doesn't need to have a timeline attached to it – it's a 'one day' dream.

Vision boards are a wonderful way to stay connected with our why. By looking daily at inspiring, beautiful images that represent the life we're striving towards, we constantly remind ourselves of the reason behind the baby steps we're taking right now. And that provides renewed faith and purpose for whatever it is we're doing.

HOW TO CREATE A VISION BOARD

Now there are entire *courses* on how to create a vision board, and some people make them into the most marvellously artistic creations, spending hours snipping images out of magazines and gluing them to a board with an assortment of trinkets, feathers, glitter and sequins for company. I bow down to these creative creatures, as I am not one of them.

The way I do my vision board *(hint: the easiest way I know how!)* is to search images online that represent my Dream Lifestyle. I save those images, then I start to collate them into a blank Powerpoint slide. By cropping, resizing and shuffling, I end up with a composite of images that perfectly capture the life I wish to be leading. I print two copies onto A4 paper and laminate them. One copy lives by my bed, the other lives in the shower. I also have my vision board as the desktop image on my computer.

I've shared my current vision board in your Step Into You Playbook (available from my website at lorrainemurphy.com.au/playbook). On the board you'll find, amongst other things, images of me and my family, my dream home office, a gorgeous meditation space, a dreamy bathroom, women I admire, a business-class plane seat, my favourite villa in Bali, and a Tesla car.

Having a vision board is the best way I know to keep me connected with the why of what I do. And that's why I strongly suggest you create one of your own!

Track your progress

Often when we're in the midst of a goal, we lose sight of the 'why'. It feels like the end result is still so very far away, and even though we've covered some ground, there's still a stretch of road ahead of us that continues right up to the horizon. We're so busy looking at where we still need to get to that we forget to glance in the rear-view mirror and celebrate how far we've come.

I experienced that feeling of overwhelm at the length of the road ahead when it came to clearing a pretty ferocious credit card debt. I was so in the weeds of paying off a thousand dollars here or there that I became deeply demotivated by the many more thousands that I still needed to clear. It would cause me to become lax about prioritising the repayments, as they seemed like drops in the ocean compared to the entire debt.

So what did I do? I tracked my progress!

I wrote the full amount of the debt in my notebook, and each time I made a repayment I subtracted it off the total amount. I remember reaching the point at which I had repaid more than I owed – and it was a wonderful encouragement. I kept repaying, kept scribbling in the amounts in my notebook, and one day, with the help of a $5,000 profit I made from selling an online program, the debt was at zero. What a feeling!!!

So what I'm saying here is this: if you're working towards a goal – particularly one that is going to take you a while to complete – start tracking your progress. Do it as basically as you need to; it didn't take much brainpower for me to track my credit card repayments in my notebook!

And on the days when you're asking yourself, 'What's the fucking point anyway?', go back to your notebook and observe the progress you've made. And remember: you didn't get this far to only come this far.

4. CURVE BALLS

Curve balls are kids getting sick, unexpected work deadlines, pets having accidents, delayed or cancelled travel plans, an urgent need with a commitment we've already made (e.g. a wedding drama and we're a bridesmaid). The COVID-19 pandemic has been one curve ball after another . . . for the entire world.

I had the Sick Kid curve ball a few weeks ago. Wade was working at his office and I was working at home, preparing for a three-hour intensive mentoring session with a mentee in the afternoon. At lunchtime, The Dreaded Call From School came: Lexi had a stomach ache and needed to be picked up. Thus ensued a frantic negotiation between Wade and me . . . and it was decided that he would take her for the afternoon. The next problem was, where. Obviously my mentee and I couldn't work to a backdrop of Lexi on the sofa with *My Little Pony* playing, so there was a hustle to figure out where this mentoring session could actually take place. I ended up going to my mentee's place, Wade stayed at home with Lexi, and the two of us felt totally thrown for the rest of the day.

Here's the thing: it is flat-out unrealistic to assume that curve balls won't happen. They will, and they do – so we need to build in strategies to mitigate them.

First off, always aim to build in some contingency to your plans – whether that's allowing for white space in your weekly calendar or adding a 'just in case' week or two onto a project timeline.

And secondly, have a Fuck-up Plan. This is what you consult when the wheels have fully come off your goals and you need to get them back on track . . . fast.

It's a simple tool. Think about all the things that *could* go wrong and create a plan for what you'll do if they do go wrong.

The Fuck-up Plan also covers you for getting back on track when you fall off the wagon with positive habits. I know for me, my food choices get *a lot* more free and easy when I go on holiday, and I usually need some kind of clean-eating reset when I get back. That's a Fuck-up Plan in its own right.

One of my mentees, Catherine, has a long-term illness that lands her in hospital for weeks at a time when her condition flares up. In the past, she has powered on through her hospital stays, using her laptop to try to keep up with work from her hospital bed. Recently we spoke about what Fuck-up Plan she might need in place for any future hospital stays, and she identified that what would actually serve her best would be to take the time to get well, maybe using it to do some gentle personal development activities like reading.

Designing your Fuck-up Plan is your opportunity to do things better, more sustainably, more productively and more efficiently next time – and it's also a chance to explore who your support team can be. Is there a trusted neighbour, colleague or friend who could step in and help out when the curve balls inevitably come your way? If the call comes from school, is there a parent who can be your backup in case you or your partner has a commitment?

5. BREAKING PROMISES TO OURSELVES

This is the really pointy end of how many of us fall off track with goals or commitments. We allow ourselves to break a promise to

ourselves, and then that habit creeps in and becomes the norm —
until ultimately, we find ourselves fully off track.

I've saved this reason until last because it lies at the very centre
of cultivating our ability to stay on track with our commitments.
Honestly, if you can get to the point where you are consistently
keeping promises to yourself, then you are 80 per cent of the way
there when it comes to staying the course to achieve your goals.

First up, I want to give you a bonus affirmation. Here it is:
I don't break promises to myself.

I would bet that most of us are more likely to break promises
we've made to ourselves than we are to break promises we've made
to other people. And that needs to shift.

I'm going to share with you two strategies to help you keep
those promises to yourself . . .

1. Start a chain reaction.
2. Create a contract with yourself.

Start a chain reaction

I bet you've got the Diana Ross song in your head now, don't you?
I know I do!

This is a simple yet staggeringly effective strategy for keeping
promises to yourself. You commit to doing something every day . . .
and then you do it. After a few days, you feel proud of yourself for
keeping the chain going. After a month, you're extremely proud of
yourself — and it's become second nature to do your thing every
day. After a couple of months, you've built a chain that you *really*
don't want to break — so you don't.

One of my friends, Stace, started a chain of her own six months ago. One day she walked 15,000 steps – and she committed to doing it every day. For *six months now* she has kept that promise to herself. If it's 8 pm, her kids are in bed and she hasn't hit her steps, she'll set off around her neighbourhood until she's hit that magic 15,000. If the weather is truly horrible, she'll walk laps of her apartment. *That's* how strongly she feels about keeping that promise to herself!

On a recent walk together I was marvelling at how committed she's been to her daily target, and she explained to me that those 15,000 steps had come to represent self-care to her – that while caring for her family, her online community and her friends, she could still make herself a priority by hitting her steps target. I loved that.

I've got a chain reaction going myself right now. For years, I had promised myself that I'd write in a journal every single day as part of my morning routine . . . but sometimes I'd sleep later, sometimes Lexi would wake earlier, or sometimes I'd skip the journalling in favour of getting stuck into my day. I swapped to writing at night, and that made me more consistent. However, I'd still miss days, due to being so tired by the time I hit our bed, or the CBF Index being high, or Wade and I having intimate time before we went to sleep.

Then one day in March 2020 I journalled at night – and decided I was going to do it every day, come late bedtimes, early starts, sickness, holidays or sex, till a chain reaction was in place.

For exactly 380 days I wrote . . . and now the habit is well and truly ingrained: I know I'm back on the chain train again.

Think about what chain reactions you could create in your life – maybe it would be to meditate, drink a green smoothie, text

a friend or read a personal development book for five minutes –
and get started!

Create a contract with yourself

The second thing you can do in order to keep a promise to yourself
is to create a contract . . . between you, and you!

I've created a template for you that is included in the playbook
you can grab from my website: lorrainemurphy.com.au/playbook.

I love this template for a few reasons:

- You're setting out, in black and white, the promise you're making
  to yourself.
- You're stating the 'why' for this promise.
- You're clearly outlining three things that will be required from
  you to fulfil this promise.
- You're tying it back to a positive, magnetic emotion.

This stuff really works! You can write just one contract to yourself,
or a contract for a handful of goals. I wouldn't do more than three,
though, as too many will just put you under pressure.

OVER TO YOU

Well, my friend, we have dived really, really deep into how you
can support yourself to stay on track with your goals, habits and
dreams. You've got a veritable shedload of tools at your disposal!
Now it's time to make them work for YOU. I believe in you. You
can do this.

Please remember:

- There are five main reasons we fall off track with goals: self-doubt, overcommitting, forgetting our 'why', curve balls and breaking promises to ourselves.
- There are specific tactics we can employ to safeguard ourselves from these pitfalls.
- We can be running toxic self-talk patterns, and be totally unaware of them.
- Affirmations are uplifting, positive statements that counteract negative self-talk.
- Vision boards can help us stay connected with our 'why'.
- Curve balls are a fact of life – and having a Fuck-up Plan ready is a powerful ally in offsetting the disruption they cause.
- The most important person to keep our promises to is ourselves.

Chapter 11

ALIGNMENT OVER BALANCE

REMEMBER WAY BACK IN CHAPTER 6 WHEN I SHARED ELIZABETH Gilbert's quote that women use the word 'purpose' like an assault weapon on themselves? Well, another way women drive themselves to distraction is with 'balance'.

Balance, and the endless pursuit of this elusive state, is the bane of many a woman's existence. We strive every day to achieve it, berate ourselves when we don't, and constantly feel guilty, stressed and even ashamed that we haven't reached that mythical Land of Balance . . . yet.

Look around you. Do you see the men in your life obsessing about the lack of balance in their lives? I'm guessing that, like me, you don't. Sure, they might say that they want to work fewer evenings, or have some more time for their hobbies or families, but they're not taking on this incredible pressure to achieve perfect balance in their lives . . . the pressure that we women get foisted upon us as soon as we emerge into the grown-up world.

In my last book, *Baby, You're Remarkable*, I got on my soapbox about the word 'juggle' as it relates to working mothers, and why it drives me so crazy.

In it I wrote:

> I can bet that whoever you dear reader are, that it is very very unlikely that you can juggle. Yet – for some unexplained reason – the moment a woman births a baby and attempts to then go back to work after having said baby, she is expected overnight to be able to juggle. Whether she ran off to the circus or not.
>
> And the worst thing, in my opinion? That *we expect ourselves* to be able to juggle!
>
> So what we have is millions of women setting themselves up every single day in a vain attempt to master a skill that – unless we book ourselves into emergency circus school or stay up late into the night for weeks on end hitting play and pause on juggling tutorial videos – we cannot master.
>
> Friends, this is lunacy.

It is also lunacy to chase the dream that one day, when work settles down, when our partner's life is less full-on, when the kids grow up, when we're getting eight hours of sleep every night, when we have the cash for the personal trainer, when we have that little nook just for us in the house, that *then* we'll live a balanced life.

It's just putting way, way, *way* too much pressure on ourselves!

So what should we focus on instead?

ALIGNMENT

I am a big fan of the concept of alignment, defined as 'a position of agreement or alliance'.

Now I don't know about you, but I would much rather live my days in a position of agreement (with myself) than I would endlessly chasing a perfect state of balance. The reason that I love the idea of aiming to live our lives in alignment is that it gives us permission to prioritise, depending on the life-season or current focus we have in our lives. This is very different to the concept of balance, which comes with an expectation that every area of our lives should be humming along at a similar rate of success: our health, our relationships, our work, our family lives, our spirituality, our finances . . .

Not possible!!

I love the way former United States Secretary of State Madeleine Albright put it during a discussion with Sandra Day O'Connor at the New York Public Library: 'I do think women can have it all, but not all at the same time. Our life comes in segments, and we have to understand that we can have it all if we're not trying to do it all at once.' Now, some people might think that's limiting to women, but I think it's 100 per cent liberating. It gives women permission to prioritise what's important to them at a particular time in their lives, instead of feeling the need to be a superhuman doing it all, all the time.

Here, in three simple steps, is how alignment works:

1. We decide what our key priorities are for a period of time.
2. We devote 80 per cent of our time and energy to those priorities.

3. *We give ourselves permission to de-prioritise the dozen other things that could/should be done during that period of time.*

In 2021, for example, my work was my major focus for the first five months of the year. I packed more into those five months than at any time previously with my business. I worked longer hours and was definitely less mentally present when I was with Wade and Lexi. I also didn't see as much of my friends as I would have liked to. The fact was that my business was my priority, and my life had to align with that.

Then, in June, I stepped back from my business for a full three months in order to go into 'Baby Land' (as I like to call it). When I undertook my annual goal-setting exercise the December before, I had committed to creating this three-month window. I remembered how hectic the first three months of Lexi's life had been, and I was determined to sink as deep and long into that special newborn bubble as I could.

I had set up everything else to work without me in that time. The team was organised, content was batched, my annual launch program had been worked around it, revenue was generated to cover the fact that there would be no program launches or events for three months, and this book was almost written.

Once Baby Land rolled around, my priority swapped to our little family – to welcoming our sweet Wilder and to helping all of us adjust to this new chapter in our lives as a family. And life fell into alignment around that. For those three months, I maintained just three parts of my business, which amounted to a total of 12 hours of 'people-facing' work and a few days of writing time.

The seasons of life

Another way of looking at alignment is through the metaphor of seasons. As I mentioned in Chapter 1, my wise friend and business coach Rachel MacDonald talks about the idea that life moves in seasons. Nothing is permanent, even if we sometimes feel stuck in a rut.

Similar ideas came up in an episode of *The goop Podcast* I recently listened to, where Katherine May, author of a book called *Wintering*, was interviewed. May discussed the need for us to accept the importance of resting and retreating during difficult times. I know I've had experiences where it's felt like everyone else is basking in their summer while all I want to do is tuck myself away in metaphorical hibernation for a few months. But you know what? I haven't always allowed myself that 'luxury'.

The thing is, we need to understand that life is just like the seasons. In nature, there's a season for the leaves to fall, there's a season for snow to fall, there's a season for little buds to pop out on trees, and there's a season for fully blooming flowers. No one season is about making all of the shit happen all at once. In the same way, life evolves and changes, and I guarantee that if you seek alignment over balance it will flow so much more easily.

So now you and I have discussed the concept of alignment . . . Let's talk about how we can recognise when something in our lives is *out* of alignment.

YOUR BODY KEEPS THE SCORE

When I was planning one of my early trips to Bali, my friend Tenielle sent me a healer's details, along with an explicit instruction that I *must* see him when I was there. Tenielle gives excellent recommendations, so I made sure I booked in a session.

Jimmy Doyle's work made such an impression on me that I have seen him on every Bali trip since, and I've sent my sister, mother, and countless friends and members of my community to him, too. He's also the healer I choose to care for my guests on my Bali retreats.

A couple of years ago, I was hosting the very first of those retreats. Jimmy was going to be visiting us to treat each of my guests, and I booked in with him myself the day before they arrived. At the beginning of the session, Jimmy abruptly asked, 'What's going on with your shoulder?' As far as I knew, both my shoulders were A-okay, but then he touched a specific spot on my left shoulder and it was *agonising*.

'Where are you feeling a burden with a woman or women?' Jimmy asked. It took me a couple of minutes, and I realised what the 'burden' was. The next day, I had nine women joining me for seven nights, and seven of them I had never met or even engaged with online before. It was my first time hosting a retreat like this, I was in a foreign country and I desperately wanted every one of those guests to have a life-changing experience.

Jimmy gave me an affirmation to repeat aloud ('I choose to allow all my experiences as a woman and with all women to be joyous and loving') while he pressed the point on my shoulder. As I repeated it, the pain began to ease, even though Jimmy told me that he was pressing harder and harder. After a couple of minutes, the pain was completely gone and I felt a lightness that wasn't there before.

This small example demonstrated to me how much our body communicates to us, and how it can help us realign our lives and ourselves. (Which is why Jimmy describes himself as a 'facilitator' because he believes his clients have the ability to heal themselves.)

Jimmy's practice is based on the work of Louise Hay. If you haven't heard of her before, you *must* read her books. She was an American healer (she passed away in 2019) who believed that every physical and mental symptom we experience in our bodies has a root cause in a negative belief we hold about ourselves.

From depression to a burn, from a dodgy hip to bad breath, everything has a belief root cause. Louise's philosophy asks us to be willing to change that core belief, and to replace it with a corrective and more empowering affirmation that essentially rewires our brains and eliminates the symptom we're experiencing. I like to think of it like a laptop – we find the virus causing the issue, get rid of it and replace it with a radically upgraded program.

I cannot tell you how many times I've consulted Louise's work to get to the bottom of something going on for me, our family or a friend. I even pull her book out mid-mentoring sessions when a mentee mentions an issue they're experiencing!

What I have learned from her philosophy is that our minds and bodies are incredibly closely linked, and that in order to heal ourselves on a physical level, we need to trace back to the origin of where that symptom is coming from. It's also incredibly empowering to be able to self-heal with her tools.

You might find it interesting that – for women – the left side of our bodies is said to relate to us as women, or our relationships and experiences with other women, while the right side of our bodies relates to our relationships with men. For men, the left side of their bodies relates to their relationships with women, and the right side relates to themselves as men, or their relationships with other men.

I'll give you some examples from my life and the lives of my mentees where Louise Hay's approach really resonated:

Example 1

- **The problem:** I had an ache and clicking in my right hip.
- **The cause:** A fear of moving forward with a male in my life.
- **The story:** At that time, Wade and I were struggling to make forward-facing plans together.

Example 2

- **The problem:** I was depressed.
- **The cause:** Anger I believed I didn't have the right to feel. (Interestingly, this came up in a session with Jimmy and I believe part of my healing was him validating that I *did* have a right to be angry about my experiences.)
- **The story:** I was telling myself that my financial stress and miscarriages weren't *that* bad, and that I should just get over them.

Example 3

- **The problem:** My mentee Liz had an attack of laryngitis.
- **The cause:** Being so mad she couldn't speak, and being fearful of speaking up.
- **The story:** Liz had an employee she had inherited from her business's previous owner who was creating a toxic environment at

work, and who Liz also found to be intimidating. Liz's episode of laryngitis happened as she was preparing to exit the team member.

Example 4

- **The problem:** Another mentee had bronchitis just before we started working together.
- **The cause:** An 'inflamed family environment', according to Louise Hay's book *You Can Heal Your Life*.
- **The story:** My mentee had been unhappy in her marriage for quite a while and had recently left home for a week to consider whether or not she wanted to continue in the relationship (and to give her partner a wake-up call!).

Example 5

- **The problem:** My friend Stace had a collapsed lung.
- **The cause:** Feelings of 'depression, grief, fear of taking in life', according to *You Can Heal Your Life*.
- **The story:** Stace and her husband had recently begun a huge renovation of their house when the builders found that three original walls were collapsing and would need to be fully replaced. This added a lot to an already hefty renovation expense.

IMPORTANT NOTE

I don't believe this form of healing is a total replacement or substitute for conventional medicine. However, I do believe that an ongoing practice of staying in tune with our bodies can act as a wonderful preventative maintenance tool to keep alignment in ourselves and in our lives, and that it can also complement whatever treatments that are recommended to us by doctors.

Now we understand how our bodies give us clues when our lives are out of alignment, let's consider what can happen when we don't find our way back into alignment.

INTRODUCING RESILIENCE FATIGUE

I first learnt of the concept of Resilience Fatigue from one of my dear friends, Jack Delosa. He created a video about it for social media, and in it he perfectly encapsulated something I had felt myself.

Let me tell you a little about Jack. Jack started The Entourage in 2010, and over the next six years it grew into Australia's largest coaching and training organisation for entrepreneurs. In 2016, a change of government policy very nearly wiped out the business. It was three months away from losing $800,000 per month and, after six years of building a team of 90, Jack had to say goodbye to 50 of them. He was meeting with liquidators. His mother's house was on the line (Jack had purchased it for her years before, and if the business went under, so would it). He was told over and over again that there was no way he could keep the business going.

But he did. It took three years of pure graft, strategic changes and hustling with his team, but the business recovered – and in fact, is now doing better than ever.

In that video he posted to social media, Jack shares some of the stresses of that period, and tells of how he was amazed when, months after the business had stabilised, an issue arose that totally floored him. The thing is, it was not a major issue. Prior to the business almost going under, it was something that wouldn't have even fazed him, but it stressed him out to the max. And then he realised why . . .

He had Resilience Fatigue.

He had pushed through fear, challenge and exhaustion for years to get his business to a safe harbour, to the point that he had no resilience left. So when this relatively minor issue arose, he simply did not have the means to deal with it.

This made so much sense to me! I could see with perfect clarity how that had happened to me, too: the sale of my first business, the interstate move, the time apart from Wade, his business challenges, trying to establish my second business, the first miscarriage. I had cashed in all my resilience cheques and I was out of credit. Then the second miscarriage occurred and it was game over for me.

I had Resilience Fatigue. And with hindsight, I can clearly see this was a major consequence of pushing through life, trying to tackle all the challenges all at once, without being able to step back and realign myself and my priorities.

THE NEED FOR RETREAT

I often speak to women who've been desperately trying to make that juggling act called 'balance' happen – keeping up their work hours, meeting all the requirements of their family, ticking the exercise boxes, staying in touch with friends and squeezing in date nights with their partners.

They're totally knackered. And they're confused. They say to me: *'But I'm doing all the things! Why am I not feeling* better *than this?'*

My first answer is to tell them about the concept of alignment and the risk of Resilience Fatigue, but if that doesn't help shift things in their lives, then I recommend a retreat – aka *a deep reset*.

I am absolutely convinced that every woman needs to get away on her own at least once a year. For my part, I would not have remained sane over the last ten years without retreats.

Now, by 'retreat' I don't mean a fancy holiday that comes with a high price tag. A retreat is simply a window of time and space that you create just for you. It can be as elaborate or as simple as you decide to make it – but it most definitely means that you only have yourself to look after for that time.

Partway through writing this book I went on a four-day retreat to Byron Bay. The pretext was to get a solid chunk of this book written before the new baby arrived. However, I also really needed to get away.

As I already mentioned, it had been a full-on few months on the business front. Additionally, Wade had had a lot of challenges with his own business, and these were not only very disruptive for him but for our household as well. I'd had three weeks and five weekends of solo parenting while he was away for work. Lexi was in the throes of threenager-dom, and the important task of laying down boundaries was proving exhausting. Oh, and there was the whole pregnancy thing, too.

I could feel resentment setting in, and irritability was starting to become part of my daily experience. I was exhausted.

So I cooked up a writing retreat in order to give myself some space and time to be in my own juices and have absolutely no-one to care for or plan around.

I booked a studio unit that backed onto a nature reserve, did a shop for delicious food at the local grocery store, and holed up for four nights. I got the writing done, and it was an enormous luxury to be able to fall fully into flow, with absolutely no distractions. But I also got to do all the things that I don't always find time or space for at home. I woke up whenever my body was ready to, I meditated in the afternoon as well as the morning, I went for walks on the beach whenever I chose to, and I used the same bowl, plate, cup, glass and cutlery for four days.

It was heavenly. And the best bit? I felt stronger, clearer, more focused, more aligned . . . and also so excited to see Wade and Lexi again, and to 're-enter' life at home.

The need for retreat brings to mind the poem 'The Grand Distraction' by Iain Thomas, which describes the world constantly dragging us by the hand, telling us what's important, what needs our attention, what we need to worry about, and how we must make a conscious effort to pull our hand back and put it on our heart – because *that*, my dear, is what is really important. And it is why, if I could, I would prescribe an annual retreat to every single woman. Getting away gives us the opportunity to put our hands back on our own hearts, and to realign our lives and ourselves when being asked to do so in the middle of everyday life seems impossible.

I've been fortunate to host a number of retreats within my business, and they are probably the most soul-nourishing part of my work.

My guests generally arrive on the first day looking frazzled, flat and a little frantic from the logistics of actually getting themselves away. Then there's a period of 'landing' into the retreat, where they realise they have sweet FA responsibilities for the next few days. I always make sure the afternoons are free so guests can have naps, read or explore the local area – essentially, have time to process whatever might be coming up for them on the retreat. Without fail, there are women who are at a total loss, on the first day, to fill four or five hours with activities just for themselves. It has been years since they have had a block of time like that.

Then they start to re-ignite. The space, the company of other women and the nurturing of the retreat . . . the insights start to drop in, clarity arrives and energy comes rushing back to them.

By the final day, they genuinely seem to be different people. It's a wonder to witness, every single time.

On the last retreat I hosted, I had a guest who had just gone through a miscarriage, another who had left her 35-year marriage a year earlier, and another who was working with her partner to get back on track after infidelity. On other retreats, there have been bankruptcies, relationship break-ups, serious health issues, bereavements . . .

However, we don't need to have experienced major life challenges like this to give ourselves a break. We don't need to be camped on the doorstep of burnout and/or breakdown. For one woman I hosted, the transformational experience she had over our four days together actually helped her support her adult daughter, when, the week after she got home, her daughter fell seriously ill. I see solo getaways as a respite from the day-to-day responsibilities of life and an insurance policy for whatever life throws at my Future Self. Retreats (be they 24 hours or 14 days long) help us to rest, realign and build up our resilience.

My biggest tips on taking a retreat

1. **Take what time you can** – it might be 48 hours, it might be ten days. Max out whatever time you can possibly take to have your retreat. It's not easy to get this time in your diary, so make the absolute most of it!

2. **Book it in ASAP** – remember in Chapter 4 when we talked about the oxytocin hit women *immediately* get when they plan something nice for themselves? This is why you want to get that booking in the diary as early as you can – you'll start feeling the benefit of your retreat before you've even left.

3. **If you can, try a guided retreat** – where someone else is doing all the thinking and planning for you. I still remember so clearly the first time I went on one myself. As I got off the bus, someone took my luggage from me, told me where to find lunch and to sit down and wait for the welcome talk. The *relief* that someone else was in charge was mind-blowing!

4. **Make it easy** – don't go getting planes or committing to long drives unless you need to. Too much travel adds more stress and it also eats into your R&R time. One of my favourite retreats is to stay at a hotel a 25-minute drive from our house. Keep it simple.

5. **Don't take work with you** – it's so tempting to take a task away that could benefit from some no-distraction time . . . But it's a

slippery slope – once you allow yourself to do one task, it makes it easier to commit to a second, and so on.

6. **Go alone** – some women love going on retreats with friends, however I feel that cheats them out of that time to really sit with themselves, to have the space to think and allow those special soul whispers to drop in. I know it can feel less daunting to go on a retreat with someone else, and it's also easy to give yourself permission to go if someone else is going too . . . but if you can, make it happen just for you.

7. **Leave the guilt at home** – as mentioned in Chapter 5, guilt erodes the value of energy boosting time like retreats. We can get so guilty about leaving our partners/kids/teams to prioritise ourselves for a few days, but they're not getting the best of us when we're stressed, shitty and frazzled with them every day. They deserve better than that. You deserve better than that.

And I firmly believe that it is healthy for our children to have time away from us. If we are mothers, we can fall into the trap of believing that our role is to protect and anaesthetise our kids from every pain and misfortune – which isn't going to serve them in their lives. I know Lexi finds it tough at times when I'm away, but she leans on her own internal resources (and the support of her dad) to move through that. And that strength is what we want for her in her life.

IMPORTANT NOTE

I know that for many women the idea of stepping out of the day-to-day for even 24 hours is a daunting thought – but it is possible. It might take serious strategising with your partner, pushing back a couple of work deadlines, drafting in some family or friends for kid-duty, saving up some cash for a few months . . . But it CAN BE DONE.

I regularly make part of my mentee's 'home play' (like homework, but more fun!) booking themselves a 24-hour staycation. And they tell me afterwards that it was the best 24 hours they've had all year.

Please remember: ~~~~~~~~~~

- The pursuit of balance can be crazy-making – seeking alignment is a much more achievable approach.
- Life comes in seasons.
- Resilience Fatigue happens when we push through too many obstacles and no longer have the resources to bounce back.
- Retreats – no matter how long they are – give us the chance to realign our lives and ourselves.
- Retreats also offer us the chance to pre-emptively build our resilience in order to deal with future challenges.

Chapter 12

ASSEMBLING YOUR SUPPORT TEAM

AS YOU ARE PROBABLY AWARE BY NOW, THIS BOOK IS ALL ABOUT stepping into you – that is to say, becoming the best version of yourself that you possibly can. So far we have walked through the processes, tools and exercises that have worked for me and that I extend to my mentees.

Let me remind you that you don't have to fly solo on this Step Into You journey. Any world-class performer will have a team of experts optimising them for success in whatever their field of excellence is. I believe that we *all* need skilful and supportive people around us to create and maintain the lives that we wish to live.

We are so fortunate to have a range of experts we can utilise in order to optimise our most important asset: ourselves. I've experimented with a lot of types of support, from business coaching to hypnotherapy, and the people I mentor frequently ask me for advice on the why, who, what and how of seeking support.

In this chapter I'm going to explore some of the different types of support we can tap into (including low cost and even free guidance). I'll share my own experiences with different modalities, and pass on the biggest lessons I've learnt when consulting with experts in different fields. Think of it as a whistlestop tour of the different support people you can consult.

You might feel you would like to utilise a certain type of support straight away, or you might keep this list in your metaphorical back pocket for when you need some extra 'oomph' in your life somewhere down the track. Whatever the case, let's dive in . . .

TALK THERAPY

For ease, I'll refer to this simply as 'therapy'. The fundamental concept of therapy is that we find clarity and peace of mind from talking through a particular experience, event or emotion with a trained expert. That expert, be she/he a psychologist, psychiatrist, counsellor or therapist, works with a specific model or protocol to help us unpack our challenges, make sense of them and find new ways of approaching life.

If, like me, you've ever wondered about the difference between a psychologist and psychiatrist, it's this: a psychologist will approach treatment with talk therapy (and maybe other elements they have trained in, like Eye Movement Desensitisation and Reprocessing), while a psychiatrist will consult through dialogue as well as prescribe medications to support mental health.

In years past there may have been taboos around 'being in therapy' or 'seeing a shrink', but today, the combination of mental health being more openly talked about and an increasing number of people seeking out talk therapy has normalised this kind of support. I have worked with two different psychologists alone, and Wade and I have engaged two different relationship therapists over the years.

Most of my friends have sought out therapy at one point in their lives at least, and I love it when someone openly shares that they see a professional with the express intention of supporting their own mental health.

It can be a big ask of a partner, family member or friend to provide a safe space for us, or to ask the 'right' questions, or to not pass judgement or be offended by our thoughts . . . never mind to be able to take an objective view when our lives and their lives are likely intimately enmeshed! So, having a safe space (or soft place to land, as my psychologist Fiona described it) to debrief on one's fears, worries and obstacles can be invaluable.

It's likely that therapy will require a commitment to regular sessions, and this can turn into a rather expensive exercise. In Australia, GPs can recommend a Mental Health Plan giving you 5–10 sessions with a psychologist, subsidised by Medicare. A tip from me: if you can, get a referral to a psychology practice that houses more than one practitioner. As with any relationship, the 'fit' between you and your psychologist is important, and you may need to try a few different practitioners before you find the right one for you. Having a referral to the broader practice means that you can switch to a different psychologist without going back to your GP for a new referral.

I want to very explicitly state that there is no 'benchmark' for needing therapy. You don't need to have had a traumatic childhood, experienced abuse or suffered any other horrific life event. If you feel like you're not coping as well as you could be with life, then that's reason enough to seek out therapy.

Therapy apps to support mental health are also on the rise, with some offering a subscription-based model. I suggest you speak to your GP about your own individual needs before deciding what support to engage.

Explore THERAPY IF:

- you need a safe place to unpack your thoughts
- you've felt 'not yourself' for an extended period of time
- there's a specific traumatic or challenging life experience that you want to find peace with

NEUROLINGUISTIC PROGRAMMING (NLP)

NLP is a specific modality that enables us to evaluate – and potentially alter – the core thoughts and beliefs that we hold about ourselves and others.

I first came across NLP on a weekend group seminar when I was 27. It was an intense two and a half days, and it marked the first time I'd ever actually sat down and thought about my life: what had happened up until that point, and where I potentially wanted to take my life in the future.

That seminar created the space for me to ask questions like:

'What are my core values?'
'What negative or limiting beliefs have I been hauling around since my childhood?'
'What past experiences have shaped my attitude to things like money, relationships, success and love?'

The experience was incredibly enlightening. My biggest realisation was that my thoughts and beliefs are not 'just who I am'. They came from almost three decades of conditioning from the people, experiences, challenges and opportunities I had navigated. I realised that I could look at some of those beliefs critically, and allow those that didn't serve me to fall away. In the words of an expression I heard a while ago: 'Don't believe everything you think!'

There were a lot of seeds planted at that seminar – including my decision to one day start my own business. Just recently (and 11 years after the seminar) I was tidying my office and came across the workbook from that weekend. Reading through the goals and intentions that I had set, I was amazed to observe just how many of them had gone on to materialise.

There are numerous tools in the NLP practitioner's kit. Most therapists include the use of emotive or suggestive language, visualisation tools, and the famous 'swish technique' (which enables us to find joy/motivation in something we didn't previously enjoy by creating an association between that task and something we *do* enjoy). You can work with a practitioner one-on-one, or in group situations like I experienced that first time. Many coaches are also

NLP-trained and use the modality to enhance their work with their clients.

An example of a high-profile NLP practitioner is Tony Robbins, whose events I have attended and got a huge amount of value from. If you can, try to attend a seminar led by a credible NLP practitioner. I've gone to a number of seminars over the years, and they have been motivating, contemplative and also entertaining experiences.

Explore NLP IF:

- you feel you've got some heavy, limiting beliefs that you can't seem to shift
- you want to get to the roots of your values
- you want to fast-track your goals

MENTORING

I've been so lucky to have many, many, many mentors, in the form of bosses, colleagues, advisory board members and friends. I would also consider my husband Wade a hugely influential mentor for me.

But what *is* a mentor? I want to be really clear on my definition of this, as there is a lot of confusion. A mentor is someone who's *been there*: they've done something you want to do or are currently attempting to do. A mentor can help you navigate the path they've already walked – including avoiding the pitfalls, finding the short-cuts and intimately knowing the challenges you face.

I like to think of it as a big forest. When we're undertaking something for the first time (becoming a parent, starting a business, finding a corporate role, creating a romantic partnership, moving overseas or interstate), the way through the forest can feel overwhelming. We don't know where to start, we don't know whether to take a left or a right turn, we can't tell when we're lost . . .

A mentor, having been there, done that and bought the T-shirt, has the benefit of being able to take a helicopter view of the forest. They can see the route through the forest that will land you at your intended destination with as little pain and anguish as possible.

Mentors have the ability to save us shitloads of time, and incalculable stress. I consulted an entire roster of mentors regularly in my first business, and I swear they helped me achieve in five years what it might take another business owner 15 years to accomplish – including annual turnover in the multi-millions and a high profile in my industry.

There are three different types of mentors:

1. Paid mentors

Paid mentors will likely have a specific mentoring offer set up, and it will be a revenue stream for them – either within their business or as a side hustle to their employment. This involves paying an agreed fee to a mentor – perhaps for a one-off or ad hoc session, or committing to a pre-agreed package of sessions.

This is where I sit. I did unpaid mentoring for several years – as part of structured mentoring programs run by third-party organisations, and also with mentees who reached out to me directly.

I enjoyed my interactions so much that I created a simple mentoring package while I was still running my first business . . . and for the first time attached a fee. The first four spots were taken within a day, and I've been a paid mentor ever since.

The great thing about paid mentoring is that you know what you're getting for your investment upfront, and as a result, the boundaries are clear. Given that there is a fee attached to a mentor's time, you also know that they have 'ring-fenced' their time and energy to work with you over your agreed period, and that you will be their priority.

I've also found that those who pay for mentoring with me magically get much better results than those who don't! I know myself that if I've invested money in something (a mentor, but equally, a gym membership), I'll make sure I max out the benefit of that investment.

2. Unpaid mentors

Unpaid mentors are likely to be drawn from a very broad base. For example, my unpaid mentors have included: friends, aunts, speakers at events I have attended, Wade, past or existing bosses, and fellow business owners. If they were further ahead of me on a path I was setting out on, then I wanted to hear how they'd done it! And I don't relegate mentors to just the business/professional realm. Parenting is one of the steepest learning curves in life for most parents – and I've tapped into more than my fair share of family and friends who seem to be nailing it a whole lot more effectively than me!

In the case of someone I didn't already have a relationship with (e.g. a speaker I admired at an event), I've stepped beyond my comfort zone to reach out to that person and ask them to join me for coffee.

We need to think about mentoring like getting married. It would be pretty damn weird if someone showed up on a first date with you and immediately dropped to their knee and asked you to marry them. It's the same for mentoring: it would be equally odd if a potential mentor said yes to a coffee and you immediately asked them to sign up to being your mentor . . .

For a few reasons:

- They don't know you from Adam or Eve.
- They have no idea yet if they can help you or not.
- They have zero clue as to what you have in mind – is it a weekly one-hour phone chat, or ad hoc coffees whenever you happen to be in the same suburb?

So – please – don't make it a bigger deal than it needs to be. I've found this approach to be much better:

- Step 1: Invite potential mentor to coffee or propose a phone call.
- Step 2: Gauge how you get on and if the mentor has the experience you're seeking to replicate.
- Step 3: At the end of coffee/call, tell them you really enjoyed it, thank them profusely, and ask if you could do it again some time.
- Step 4: Always, *always* send a thank you card afterwards.

This approach makes it easy for both sides to engage, as it's informal and doesn't put any time or energy pressure on someone who is likely to have a tighter schedule than we do ourselves.

The fact that it's not paid means that we can (in theory!) have multiple mentors we're seeking advice from at any time, and that no-one is tied to an arrangement that may not suit them.

The challenge I have found with unpaid mentoring (as a mentee) is that I am patently conscious of 'taking up' the mentor's time. As there is no fee structure in place, I have sometimes not taken a particular issue or challenge to a mentor because I would have felt bad placing a demand on their already stretched time.

And – on the other side of the table – an issue I've found with this arrangement as an unpaid mentor is that when my business gets busy, I simply can't prioritise my mentees beyond the agreed times we'd set to talk.

3. Stealth mentors

Some mentors don't necessarily even know we exist. Sounds strange, right?! However, there are many people that I would consider a mentor to me . . . and I've never met them. In this group of what I call 'stealth mentors' are authors of books that have helped me, people I follow on Instagram, and speakers at events.

Many thought-leaders have been hugely generous in compiling and then sharing their knowledge and expertise in the form of content that is free (social media, email newsletters, free ebooks and trainings like webinars) or low cost (books, events). We can access this content for a tiny percentage of what it would cost to work with that person one-on-one. Think about it: to work with Tony Robbins himself I would probably need to invest at least a million dollars. However, I can binge on his books, trainings and events for a comparatively tiny sum.

This book that you're reading is a summary of the ideas, tools and exercises that have been most powerful for my mentees. Now, I know that you and I aren't sitting here one-on-one together, but I've shared a *lot* in this book.

So remember, if your budget doesn't stretch to a paid mentor, or if seeking out unpaid mentors doesn't suit your priorities, time or energy at the moment, you can still access the work of thousands of experts – right where you are.

Explore MENTORING IF:

- you're at a crossroads and want a trusted person's input
- you're on a new path and want to fast-track your success on it
- your motivation is lagging and you need a boost

COACHING

The next option for your support team is a coach. I do need to flag at the outset that there can be a lot of overlap between mentoring and coaching. How I differentiate the two is this:

- **Mentoring** is the support of someone who's been on the path you're on and has achieved something you want to achieve. Mentoring can be paid, unpaid or acquired at low cost.
- **Coaching** involves an infrastructure of concepts, exercises or approaches to help you achieve an outcome. The coach hasn't necessarily achieved that outcome him- or herself. Coaching is paid support.

The overlap occurs when a mentor (most likely a paid mentor) has developed his or her own bank of resources over time, like a coach would. (I, for example, have got a pretty comprehensive toolkit that I employ to help my mentees.)

There is a coach for every domain you could think of: life coaches, business coaches, performance coaches, spirituality coaches, communication coaches, health coaches, sex coaches, intimacy coaches, parenting coaches, writing coaches, meditation coaches, presentation coaches, organisation coaches . . . I could go on!

In the process of building my businesses, I have engaged with many coaches over the years, both via group coaching programs and in one-on-one sessions. I've also engaged coaches for non-professional areas of my life, including health coaching and a parenting coach. I have sought them out for their knowledge of the area I want to improve on, and the tools that they could share with me, and discovered that, as with any industry, there are kick-ass coaches, average coaches and decidedly crap coaches.

When seeking a coach, my advised approach is:

- Step 1: Seek word-of-mouth referrals from people you trust and who have seen results with their coach.
- Step 2: Seek out the directories of professional associations or accreditation bodies of coaches to find a pool from which to shortlist from.
- Step 3: Do your research on the coach's offer and see if their philosophy resonates with you.

- Step 4: If it does, reach out to the coach for an initial conversation to evaluate whether or not the 'fit' is there for you with their skills, values and personality.
- Step 5: Get clear on the time and money involved, and check that it works for your schedule and budget.

When deciding whether or not to work with someone, keep front of mind the outcome you want to achieve. I reached out to a business coach a few years ago based on a friend's recommendation, and had an initial phone conversation with her. At the time, I wanted to make a big leap with the revenue I was making in my business, and so reviewing my business's pricing was something I needed to do. When the coach shared her fees with me, I was struck by how low they were . . . and it planted a seed of doubt for me. If she was charging low fees herself, how would she be able to support me in big fee increases for my services? I decided not to go ahead with the coaching.

Coaches don't need to have achieved the specific outcomes you have in mind; however, they do need to demonstrate that they walk their own talk in how they carry themselves in their lives, relationships and businesses.

Explore COACHING IF:

- you have a specific area of your life that you want to improve
- you feel you have ongoing blocks with making certain changes in your life
- you want to access the next level of mastery in a life area

RAPID TRANSFORMATION THERAPY (RTT)

RTT combines aspects of hypnotherapy, NLP, psychotherapy and Cognitive Behaviour Therapy (CBT). While the technique is grounded in hypnotherapy, which relies heavily on positive reinforcement, RTT goes deeper to identify what caused your patterns or limiting beliefs to form in the first place. An RTT practitioner will also create a personalised transformational recording, which you can listen to for a prescribed period of time.

The net effect is that you pull out the negative beliefs at the roots (the events that originally created them) and rewire your brain with more positive, empowering beliefs.

The first time I had RTT, I was freaking out about how I'd feel under hypnosis. I am quite the control freak, and the idea of relinquishing that control, even to someone I trusted, was deeply uncomfortable for me. I don't think it helped that TV hypnotists were a big deal when I was a kid and that they created entire shows based on humiliating their poor subjects!

As it turned out, I found the experience of being under hypnosis deeply relaxing – like a deep meditation, or how I feel in Savasana at the end of a yoga class.

Explore RTT IF:

- you can see an ongoing negative pattern in your life that you want to rewire
- something is constantly triggering a strong negative emotion (e.g. shame, sadness, embarrassment)

- you know that a negative belief is holding you back from achieving a goal (e.g. starting a business or finding a loving partner)

KINESIOLOGY

Kinesiology is a form of support that I frequently get asked about, and it's the modality that I have leaned on most consistently over the years. It is definitely one of the more 'broad-spectrum' modalities, as kinesiologists will often blend different influences and modalities, and they can work very differently to each other. I've worked with three kinesiologists over the years, and each has been unique in their approach.

According to the Australian Kinesiology Association, the goal is to identify the 'cause of any imbalance and then resolve it'. This cause may be 'nutritional, emotional, structural, psychological, energetic, or even spiritual'.

I love this style of support because it keeps me aligned across all the different areas of my life.

I've seen my kinesiologist, Jacqui Prydie, for ten years now, and for most of those years I've had a session with her every month. This means that each month I'm getting a clearing – and often negative beliefs come up in the sessions while they're still at a subconscious level. This ensures that I don't start acting out those beliefs on a conscious level . . . also known as self-sabotaging!

Explore KINESIOLOGY IF:

- you feel your mindset and/or energy are heavy, and you can't shift the feeling
- you're in the midst of making changes in your life and want to ensure you're not self-sabotaging
- you want a spiritual and energetic 'declutter'

ENERGY WORK

The energy-work space is a very broad one, encompassing reiki, massage and acuenergetics. There is a belief (that I subscribe to) that all of us are energy workers, because we're putting out our energy, interacting with other people's energy and also receiving other people's energy constantly, day to day.

I see this very clearly in my own work. Often at the beginning of a mentoring session I can tell that my mentee's energy is flat. As our session continues, I can see their energy gradually building, and by the end of our time together they seem to have had an energy transfusion. I can see this visibly if we're in person or talking over Zoom, however it's also patently apparent in their voice if we're speaking on the phone.

It's difficult to manage your energy well if you're weighed down with negativity or heaviness. Our bodies also store the memory of traumatic or challenging experiences, and over time that muscle memory can build up to create physical pain in a certain area.

I recommend engaging an energy worker as part of your support team because – as we've discussed already – effective energy management is the key to creating and joyfully living the life you dream of.

Explore ENERGY WORK IF:

- you've got niggling physical pain that hasn't been resolved by other means (e.g. physiotherapy)
- you feel hyped up or wired, and can't seem to access a more relaxed state
- you're having problems with your sleep

PSYCHICS

This is not going to be for everyone. Personally, I believe in other realms, dimensions and past lives . . . I'm there for it *all*! My thinking is this: if intuitive/spiritual support is there, why *wouldn't* you take it?

I saw psychics when I was in my twenties, more from a place of curiosity and enjoyment than as a quest for support. In the last ten years, however, I have taken the space more seriously. I've tapped into trusted psychics for guidance on my businesses, relationships and spirituality.

Psychics may just do readings and answer specific questions, but it's more likely that they'll use certain divination methods – for example, tarot cards, palm reading, muscle testing, pendulums, oracle cards and energy readings.

I will consult the psychics I work with when I'm approaching a new life or business chapter, if I'm trying to make sense of a challenging experience (for example, our miscarriages) or if I want input into a decision I'm trying to make. At other times, life is just difficult and I'm seeking reassurance that things will improve.

Explore PSYCHIC SUPPORT IF:

- you want reassurance that you're on the right path
- you want to cover all bases before making a key decision
- you're trying to make sense of a life curve ball

My intention with this chapter has been to provide a mini-directory of the support modalities that might help you right now, or in future. Explore as many or as few as you like. Remember that there is always a host of options available to guide you on your own unique path.

When choosing a practitioner, consider the following advice . . .

HOW TO FIND THE RIGHT EXPERT FOR YOU

As I mentioned already, in any space there will be brilliant practitioners, average ones and downright rubbish ones. So I want to set you up for success if you do seek out the help of experts. Here's what to consider:

- **Word of mouth is queen** – Ask people you trust who they work with. In my experience, recommendations rarely lead to negative experiences.

- **Do your research** – Check out a practitioner's website, their social media channels and, if appropriate, ask to speak to existing clients of theirs.
- **Check in with your gut** – Always, always listen to your gut on whether or not working with someone will be in your best interests. I've overridden my gut a few times in this situation, and it's always resulted in wasted time, energy, money and expectations. *Remember: if it's not a 'hell yes!' it's a no.*
- **Check the fit** – Obviously, you need this person to have the know-how and experience to help you, but the personality fit is also key. Particularly in the instance of mentoring or coaching, you're likely to be working with this person intimately, and that gets very difficult if you don't gel together. I'm not saying you need to be their best friend, but you should be able to build enough of a rapport to help you achieve your goals.
- **Check for trust** – Remember that this person is going to have access to your thoughts, energy and, depending on the practitioner, your finances and relationships. You absolutely must trust them!
- **Dip your toe in** – It makes sense to trial working with a new practitioner for a session or two before committing to a package with a hefty price tag or a lengthy time investment.

ON EXPECTATIONS

There are a few common pitfalls you may experience as you assemble your support team. To set you up for max success, here are some key pointers.

1. Share your desired outcome upfront

When you're discussing with a practitioner the possibility of working with them, be very honest as to what your expectations are. This forces you to get clear on what success looks like, and it also gives the practitioner an opportunity to evaluate whether or not they can help you, and what a realistic budget and time frame would be to achieve your outcome.

Last year, I had an initial consultation with my acupuncturist, Maggie Godin. Based on her assessment, she told me she would need to see me every week for eight weeks in order to get the health result I wanted. I had envisaged a couple of sessions sorting me out, so this was a surprise, and I was also looking at a significant financial and time commitment. Going back to my own checklist, my gut was a 'hell yes' and I trusted Maggie, so I committed to the work with her. And I'm very happy I did.

2. Be wary of too many opinions

In recommending the eight modalities that I have in this chapter, I am not saying that you must jump online and book yourself in with eight different practitioners. Far from it! I've seen some women in my community enlist the support of every expert available, and they're simultaneously working on a business overhaul, financial attunement and spiritual uplevelling with various experts. Be mindful of listening to too many voices at once, and of overriding your own innate guidance with the input of others. I don't work with all of these experts all of the time; instead, I switch on/off and dial up/down the support that I feel I need at any particular time.

3. Stay in the room

'The work', whether it's energy work, mentoring or hypnotherapy, is unlikely to make a huge impact immediately. Many of the modalities I've covered in this chapter involve deep work – whether that's uprooting negative beliefs we've hauled around for decades, or addressing energy imbalances. We're not after cosmetic bandaids; we want intensive, lasting, transformational change. And that can take time.

My measure for whether the work is benefitting me or not is if I feel somewhat better after a session. If I do, that's my cue to 'stay in the room' and keep doing the work.

That said . . .

4. Don't persist if it's not helping

I don't believe we should push through indefinitely if the work isn't helping. There *is* a practitioner out there who will be a brilliant support for you . . . it just may not be the person you're working with right now. I truly believe the reason I've built such a stellar 'little black book' of practitioners is that I've moved on quickly when it became clear that a particular support person wasn't working out. So don't be afraid to move on if the relationship isn't serving you.

Please remember: ～～～～～～～～～～～～～

- Just like world-class performers, we all need a support team around us to help create the lives we wish to be living.
- A mentor is someone who has already walked the path you're on.

- A coach will work through an infrastructure of concepts, exercises or approaches to help you achieve an outcome.
- Kinesiology can help us clear self-sabotage on a subconscious level.
- Word-of-mouth referrals from someone you trust is the most reliable way to find an expert to support you.
- Your gut feel is an important element in deciding to work with an expert (or not!).
- There is a huge amount of content out there at low to no cost via social media, books and online programs, which are an excellent place to start as you educate yourself on which modalities will support you best.

Part 5

The hotspots

My intention in this section is to unpack the three taboo areas
I find women struggle with most, and normalise talking about
them, so that you can create success within them in your life.

Chapter 13

ESTABLISHING BOUNDARIES

TIME TO ROLL UP OUR SLEEVES AND ADDRESS THE FIRST OF THREE hotspots together!

If you're someone who finds it difficult to set boundaries in your life, please don't think you're alone. This is an issue that most women – me included – struggle with day to day. Here are some examples of what I hear very frequently in my community:

> *'I just don't know how to say no.'*
> *'It's easier to keep doing X than rock the boat.'*
> *'I find it really hard not to overcommit myself.'*

No-one teaches us what boundaries are or how to actively observe them in our lives. And – as I mentioned back in Chapter 1 – not many of us had mothers who role-modelled healthy boundaries to us, simply because the concept of boundaries was so far removed from the reality of our mothers', grandmothers' and great-grandmothers' lives! If a woman from those generations had been a boundary-setter, you can imagine the perception society would have had of her: 'difficult', 'selfish', 'crazy' come to mind . . .

So you and I are effectively trailblazers in this area, which is why it's not surprising that we can find it challenging. I believe there are a few other reasons why we women in particular find boundaries hard:

- **We want to be liked** – the need to be loved is our most fundamental human need, and we can feel that putting boundaries in place will make others not like us.
- **We're conditioned to people-please** – no prizes for guessing this one!
- **We might not like confrontation** – setting a boundary may involve an intimidating confrontation, and that's something that's uncomfortable at best, and agonising at worst.

Given these reasons, it can sometimes feel easier to avoid any awkward, boundary-setting conversations. But navigating those conversations and setting boundaries in place is a life skill we need to master (sorry, you're not getting off the hook that easily!) because a life without boundaries looks something like this:

- an inability to stay on track with our commitments to ourselves
- a sense of self-loathing due to our perceived 'weakness'
- a lack of clarity on what a successful day looks like
- a sense that our work is never done
- a constant feeling of overcommitment

- life feeling like a free-for-all
- a belief that our needs come last

As you can probably guess, I'm most definitely not a fan of living our one precious life this way! Now, let's look closer at why boundary-setting skills are so important.

WHY BOUNDARIES ARE CRUCIAL

When Lexi was three, (and, now I think about it, ever since!) her boundary testing was off the charts. Wade and I were both feeling very 'challenged', so we had a session with a parenting coach, who explained that all children are born to test the limits. By Lexi testing limits, she's leaning on us and other caregivers to teach her when and how a boundary has been reached, then she will modify her behaviour accordingly.

The coach went on to say that testing limits isn't something we grow out of as adults. We're constantly testing the limits because we want to know where our boundaries lie. So, if we project forward to life beyond childhood, it stands to reason that adults will at some stage test their limits with us. We need to recognise that this happens and be proactive about it, because it's up to us to hold the line when we feel a boundary of ours has been pushed too far or straight up ignored.

Another reason we need to master and maintain boundaries is that the strength, happiness and quality of our lives – and the lives of our loved ones – is very much dictated by the limits that we have in place within us and around us. Believe me, the most happy, free, successful and contented people I know have rock solid boundaries in place. Author and entrepreneur Danielle LaPorte nailed it in this line from her website: 'open, gentle heart, big fucking fence'.

A big reason for this is that an effective boundary has the power to set off a positive ripple effect in our lives – with each subsequent ripple adding more upside to our day to day. For example, you might decide to put a boundary around work emails – you don't check them after clocking off, not even to peek at them on your phone. This gives you time to properly decompress from the busyness of the working day with a walk or meditation (first ripple), which then means you feel present to enjoy family time over dinner (another ripple), which allows you to come back to work fresh the following morning (yet another ripple).

TYPES OF BOUNDARIES AND HOW TO SET THEM

I like to think about boundaries in the context of a metaphorical sandpit. I'm sitting in my sandpit, building sandcastles, but sometimes people in the sandpits around me chuck pebbles or twigs into mine, or even come right into my sandpit and flatten my sandcastles. I can't keep my sandpit up to the standard I want it to be if I don't clearly tell them to stop it. Think of your life as a sandpit – are others messing with your sand? If so, you need stronger boundaries.

Often, we only think about boundaries relating to the people around us, that is, our *extrinsic* boundaries, but it's important to recognise that we must have boundaries with ourselves, too, because the truth is, sometimes we make a mess of our own sandpits. These are called *intrinsic* boundaries.

1. Intrinsic boundaries

Boundaries begin with us. If we can't observe the boundaries we set for ourselves, what hope do we have of getting other people to observe our extrinsic boundaries? Intrinsic boundaries are an active demonstration of our self-leadership, and they include what we give our energy to, which friends we choose to spend time with and what opinions we choose to take on board.

It's important to note that self-leadership doesn't need to be restrictive or militant. I love the idea that discipline equals freedom. The more discipline we have around our boundaries, the more freedom we can go and create. To give you an example from my life, I don't watch TV from Monday to Thursday. That discipline means I sleep better, which means I have more energy during the week and then really relish the freedom to enjoy TV on the weekend.

Sleep presents us with a wonderful opportunity to finetune how disciplined we are with our intrinsic boundaries. How easy it is to say yes to that third coffee in the afternoon, to let Netflix autoplay the next episode of a show we're binging on and stay up another hour, or to do the death-scroll through social media to delay getting off the sofa rather than going to wash our faces of an evening.

I've done the bedtime struggle for *years*. I would 'commit' to being asleep by 9.30 pm, and marvel at how the hell it was 10.30 pm *again* when I was switching off the light. That missed hour of sleep made it infinitely more difficult to make my Miracle

Morning happen the next day, and I was just generally annoyed with myself.

When our second baby, Wilder, arrived, I kept up my too-late-to-bed routine . . . until it became a real pain point in my life. I got tired of being tired, and – when I was ready to build my strength again – sick of missing out on morning exercise. So, I set myself a boundary of being in our bedroom by 8 pm, and of being asleep by 9 pm. I did it and I'm already seeing the ripple effects. This morning, as I'm writing these words, I was up before both little people and fitted in 20 minutes of meditation and a 30 minute at-home barre class before they surfaced from their slumber. That secured me my precious quiet time, unlocked energy for the day ahead, and gave me that sense of fulfilment at ticking off both my daily mindfulness and exercise goals.

You'll already have your own boundaries in place. Some of them are probably working brilliantly for you right now. But there might also be some that you want to improve. Or perhaps you're thinking you've got no boundaries around your social media consumption, or sleep, or work hours. If you've got a pain point in your life – maybe it's your energy levels during the day, your productivity or your relationships – ask yourself: is there a boundary I could put in place to help negate that pain point?

2. Extrinsic boundaries

A woman who attended a retreat with me last year had recently separated from her husband of 35 years, but they still worked together and saw each other every day in the office. He was struggling to let her go, and was calling and messaging her at any time of day or night, on the pretext of having a work conversation. She put the following boundary in place: he could only call her about work during the day Monday to Friday – which enabled her to move on in this exciting new chapter of her life.

This is an excellent example of an extrinsic boundary, though these kinds of boundaries don't always have to relate to specific people – yours may relate to commitments or an entity of some form. As a straightforward rule of thumb, if you're feeling angry, resentful, taken advantage of, unheard, taken for granted or disrespected, then I guarantee you there's an extrinsic boundary that's either not in place or is too weak for your needs.

It's not always easy to set boundaries with others, but we need to remember that the initial short-term pain of having that Difficult Conversation is worth it for the long-term gain of our own peace of mind and our release from negative feelings like anger and resentment. If you don't set necessary boundaries with the people around you, if you keep going the way you're going, what will life look like in a year, five years, ten years? The quality of your life is determined by the number of Difficult Conversations you're prepared to have – which is why those successful and happy people I mentioned earlier are so adept at creating boundaries in their lives!

I created a masterclass specifically on this topic, and I called it Guts and Grace. Guts as it takes courage to strike out for ourselves and put in place that boundary with others, and grace as we want to navigate setting those boundaries with kindness – for others, but also for ourselves.

To help you with setting (and maintaining!) boundaries, I've created the 'Five Cs'. Remember these when having those Difficult Conversations:

- Calm – set the emotional benchmark for how the conversation is going to go
- Concise – avoid potential confusion by minimising fluff/extra information
- Clear – be really, really clear on what you want to happen
- Committed – stay the course and remember exactly *why* you want this boundary
- Consistent – this is where the real work lies, no matter what comes your way, hold the line on your boundary

This requires some courage. I promise you, though, the first step is the hardest part and it *does* get easier over time as you consistently stick with your boundaries. Using your boundary as a kind of mantra, or writing it down on a sticky note at the front of your notebook or putting it on your bathroom mirror, can be really helpful as these reminders act as an anchor for you even in the midst of stormy seas.

Remember that we only get one sandpit, and that sandpit is determined by the decisions we're making each day. Have a think about how some new or improved boundaries could help you protect your sandpit so you can create the life you want to create – whether that's a business, a successful career, a family, or more health, wealth or happiness. If we don't have the boundaries that we need to have in place, then we really do hold ourselves back from making that life a reality.

Please remember: ~~~~~~~~~~~~~~~~~~~~~

- It's more common than not to struggle with boundaries.
- Life without boundaries can feel like a free-for-all.
- We have a natural propensity from childhood to test boundaries.
- Having an effective boundary creates a positive ripple effect in our lives.
- There are two types of boundaries: intrinsic boundaries and extrinsic boundaries.
- Intrinsic boundaries represent our ability to self-lead.
- Extrinsic boundaries relate to our interactions and commitments with others.
- Discipline equals freedom.
- The quality of our lives is determined by the number of Difficult Conversations we're prepared to have.
- Use the Five Cs when establishing boundaries with others.

Chapter 14

BUILDING A POSITIVE MONEY MINDSET

THIS CHAPTER IS ALL ABOUT BUILDING AN ABUNDANT MONEY mindset. Over the next pages I'll share the story of my own money mindset journey, and pass on the insights, nuggets and a-ha! moments that have helped me.

I want to set the parameters very clearly for this chapter: this is not a how-to-get-rich-quick guide, or a step-by-step financial plan. This is about getting your money *mindset* in the right place – because, as I've learnt, you can have the best financial advisors in the world and they'll be FA help to you if you're going to self-sabotage anyway.

But first, why this chapter?

When women are financially empowered it enables them to be empowered across every area of their lives. And women with money can change the world.

Let's remember that I as the writer of this book and you as one of its readers are in a small global minority of women who have the privilege, the education and the means to access books like this one. Not to mention the ability to work, vote, move freely and choose our life partners. The more money you and I can generate, the more we have to share with women who are not as fortunate as we are.

So it would be remiss of me to not include this vitally important topic for you on your Step Into You journey.

WHY MONEY IS A HOTSPOT

To begin, have a quick check-in with yourself and answer these questions. How did you feel when I mentioned money? Did you feel excited? Anxious? Curious? Wary? Afraid? Neutral?

Money is one of the most sensitive topics of discussion for many people, whether it induces a positive or negative response.

I find that talking about money can be especially charged for women, and that's due to two reasons:

1. We don't talk about it

If I gave Wade a list of ten of his male friends, I believe he could tell me to the nearest $20,000 what that guy earns. He'd probably also have the inside track on his friends' investments, financial losses and goals. When I hear him on the phone to a friend, I'm conscious of how men discuss money in very transactional, non-emotional ways.

Women, on the other hand, rarely talk about money. Since my female friends and I moved beyond that first-job-out-of-uni phase,

I don't know what they earn. Money rarely, if ever, comes up in our conversations, unless it is to give or seek emotional support with a financial worry, or to make a passing reference to a salary increase, bonus earned or business target hit.

As a result, money for many women is shrouded in secrecy. Financial conversations almost veer into taboo territory. We have no benchmark for identifying what a 'good' or 'bad' financial situation is, we don't knowledge-share around finances, and so the issue of money becomes even more confusing and emotionally charged.

2. Having access to or influence around money is a relatively new phenomenon

We don't need to cast our minds back too many generations to find a time when women had zero financial independence. I would imagine, for most of us, that our grandmothers were entirely financially dependent on their husbands. That's only two generations ago!

There are obviously a host of issues women still experience as a hangover from these generations of dependency on male financial dominance (the gender pay gap being just one). But for those of us who *are* living in an era and a society that allows for us to have our own money, we are in the minority when it comes to women globally – and for that I am a) incredibly grateful, but also b) motivated to help women who don't have the freedoms I have.

MY MONEY RELATIONSHIP HISTORY

I would describe myself as having a very positive relationship with money. I started working weekends at the age of 14 and was pretty much financially self-sufficient from that time forward. Throughout my university degree I worked two jobs and also had a side hustle tutoring high school kids.

I first felt the pinch financially when I moved from my native Dublin to London, where I had to adjust to higher living expenses. However, as all of my friends were in the same £2-bottle-of-wine boat together, it wasn't too difficult to manage.

Three years after moving to Sydney in my early twenties, I had saved a solid nest egg. This enabled me to start a business and support myself financially for the first five months until the company could pay me a salary – and I have paid myself every single month since then for my nine years of being self-employed.

That first business became a big financial success, to no-one's greater surprise than my own. We turned over multi-millions of dollars a year, and I was able to treat my brilliant team to adventures like hot-air ballooning and visiting Uluru, as well as give them surprise bonuses.

I sold that business in late 2017. I was flying high financially: I bought our car outright and put a deposit down on a first home for Wade, Lexi and me. The same day I paid the house deposit I received a letter from the tax office informing me that a tax return from 2015 had been investigated and that I now owed a hefty (I'm talking six figures) amount.

(Backstory: I had engaged a specialist grant company to apply for a grant on my business's behalf three years earlier, and it turned out they were a shonky operation. The tax office retrospectively decided that our grant application didn't qualify, reversed the tax relief it had afforded the company and lumped a staggeringly harsh penalty on top for good measure.)

The amount was owed by the business I had just sold, and as I didn't think it fair to burden the new owner with that debt, I took it on personally.

As all of my money was now tied up in the house purchase, my parents offered to loan me two-thirds of the tax bill – and after months of liaising with the tax office, that gave me leverage to reduce the amount owed somewhat.

I had sold my first business, was just about to start my second one, I had committed to a sizeable mortgage, and now I owed my parents an eye-watering large amount of money. And – just like that – my money story was fucked. Totally fucked.

Over the following two years, all my financial confidence dissipated. I made most decisions around money from a place of fear and scarcity (N.B. not a good thing when you're building a business!). I worried incessantly about having enough money. It was absolutely exhausting, contributed significantly to my mental health issues, and placed a strain on my relationship.

Perhaps worst of all, I felt like an utter fraud as a mentor. Who was I to advise people on how to build successful businesses if I couldn't succeed in managing my own finances? The other ouchy point was that I *knew* I could do better. I *knew* I was capable of having an abundant money mindset, and hated that I had allowed myself to slip into such a negative, disempowered place.

After two years of money misery, I pulled on my Big Girl Pants and got seriously intentional about turning around my financial situation.

What you'll find in this chapter is the full recipe that I used to get my money mindset back to a place of abundance. You can implement many of the steps I share right now, today. And most of them cost absolutely nothing. Honestly, if I can haul my sorry, shameful ass out of the financial hole I was in, you can too.

After every setback is a comeback.

THIRTEEN STEPS TO AN ABUNDANT MONEY MINDSET

I want to share with you some snapshots of my financial comeback, not to gloat but to show you that it *is* possible to turn around your financial situation.

In the last year I have:

- brought in the same revenue in three months that I had brought in in the entire previous year
- cleared a total of $30,000 of credit card debt – and haven't paid interest since
- made up a full year of superannuation contributions in two months
- set aside $30,000 of savings to give me peace of mind going into my maternity leave
- made $60,000 in a week in my business

So you see, this stuff works! Now let's get started on the steps you can take to foster an outlook that allows you to achieve whatever financial goal you have in mind.

1. Be ready to change

Sometimes change can be prompted by the vision of a better situation (aka the carrot) and sometimes by the pain of one's current situation (aka the stick). For me, motivation came in the form of the stick!

I hit a pain barrier with my finances: the physical reaction every time I checked my credit card balance online, the gnawing pain in my stomach when I didn't hit a financial target in the business, the anxiety whenever Wade and I discussed money . . . I just got so OVER IT, I knew it needed to change. And, importantly, *I was ready to change.*

A key part of being ready to change is accepting that your finances are as they are. For me, that acceptance extended to acknowledging that what the dodgy grant company had done was on no level okay, but blaming them and continuing to play the victim wasn't serving me. In fact, it was holding me back.

Coming to terms with your money situation is Step 1 to your comeback.

2. Become aware of your money stories

Our response to all things financial is governed by our money stories. We tell ourselves stories about everything in our lives, and money is no exception. We create money stories in our childhoods, learn them off friends and absorb them from the media.

Money mindset coach Denise Duffield-Thomas pointed out that for many of us our very first experience of money is being told by adults not to touch it or put it in our mouths. So our first perception of money is that it's dirty, something to be avoided.

We may be conscious of our money stories. For example, entrepreneur Barb de Corti, founder of ENJO, a cleaning product company with a multi-million dollar revenue, was recently a guest speaker for my Mastermind group. She shared just how limiting the money story she grew up with was – she was born into a farming family, and a daily struggle for money was part of life for her parents. To attain the success she now enjoys, Barb had to – in her own words – 'unlearn a lot of beliefs'.

We can have stories that serve us well in our relationship with money, or stories that hold us back from abundance in our lives – and those negative stories can also be what money mindset mentor Denise Duffield-Thomas calls 'money blocks'.

For me, becoming aware that I was carrying a lot of excess-baggage money stories, and acknowledging how much they were holding me back, was the second step on my financial comeback. Some of my blocks included:

> *'I'll never clear this credit card, so what's the point in even trying?'*
> *'My business will never make enough money for me to get ahead.'*
> *'I don't have enough money to donate to causes I care about.'*
> *'It's pointless trying to make money as it all got taken away from me last time.'*
> *'It's shameful that I owe my parents money at my age.'*

I could probably write 30 of these, but you get the picture!

The important thing to remember is that we are never 'done' with having money blocks. Just like the layers of an onion, we peel one money block away and another presents itself. So while I've done a lot of work on becoming aware and pushing through my money blocks, there is always more work to do – and sometimes the same block keeps showing up like a pesky mosquito that just won't clear off.

Remember also that it's very easy to take on the money blocks of others – whether that's the boss who believes it's impossible to make money owning a business, the partner who refuses to spend money on investments, or the friend who regularly has a night out, courtesy of their credit card. The closer these people are to us, the more difficult it is to differentiate what blocks are theirs and what blocks are ours – and therein lies the work!

3. Go all-in on gratitude

I've long been an active cultivator of gratitude in my life. However, when I was trying to turn my money mindset around I realised how much ungratefulness had crept into my life. I had spent so much time lamenting what I *didn't* have that I'd failed to appreciate what I *did* have.

It's Oprah 101: what we appreciate appreciates. And I love her famous quote, 'Be thankful for what you have; you'll end up having more. If you concentrate on what you don't have, you will never, ever have enough.'

So, Step 3 in building an abundant money mindset is to go all-in on gratitude. Every time you notice yourself having a thought around scarcity ('I have no new clothes to wear out this weekend', 'I'm not being paid as much as my colleague'), interrupt that negative thought pattern by instead identifying some of the things you *do* have ('I've got an entire wardrobe full of clothes', 'I get to earn my own money').

I also list the five things I'm most grateful for every night before I go to sleep, and Wade and I have kept gratitude journals for each other for the last couple of years. Finding a gratitude practice that works for you will keep you on the abundance track. I'm certain that retraining my brain from a scarcity mindset to a gratitude one was – and still is – a major lever in my economic recovery.

4. Focus on what you *can* do

If your money story is as bruised and battered as mine was, it's likely that you're feeling overwhelmed by the scale of the task ahead of you. It's also likely that you'll be dependent on the actions or decisions of others – e.g. your manager approving your raise, or a partner getting on board with your plan. And, as we've seen in recent years, external circumstances that upset our financial apple cart can and do happen. There's nothing like a global pandemic to put the squeeze on financially!

We could easily spend all day worrying about the 'will they/won't theys', the 'what-ifs' and the 'if this happened, thens', but to do so is just to waste time, energy and mental calories. It's disempowering and it roots us in inertia.

What's a *much* better approach is to focus on what we *can* control and influence. My friend and fellow entrepreneur Sabri Suby recently said to me that the one thing we can control is the amount of effort we put into something – no-one and nothing can take that away from us.

You may not be able to turn your financial situation around overnight. There may be key stakeholders who aren't jumping on the bandwagon with you. Hell, you might have no clue what you're even going to do! But you can choose where you focus your energy, and that will deliver you into an empowered, motivated state. Which is precisely where you need to be.

For me, that meant getting ruthless about the number of projects and revenue streams I was creating in my business, and making the few that I did commit to work as hard as they possibly could.

5. Take positive forward action

If we don't move forward we'll stay forever stuck in a rut. So the next step to an abundant money mindset is to take positive forward action ... consistently. It's easy to get scared when there are big goals to tick off, difficult conversations to have or our own ingrained behaviour to change.

What you must remember, though, is that Person A who is afraid and Person B who appears to be brave feel the exact same emotion: fear. The difference between the two is what they do because, the fact is, if we're going to make some big shifts in our finances, we must expect to *do some new shit*.

For me, I knew that investing in paid social media ads would grow my community, increase awareness of my offers and ultimately help my business make more money. However, I had a deep-seated, probably irrational, fear of putting my face in Facebook and Instagram ads. It brought up a whole ton of self-doubt: 'Who do I think I am?', 'People will think I look stupid', 'I'm going to look pushy' ... But I knew I would never expand my business if I didn't venture into advertising and that I just had to get over it. I engaged a social media ad expert, briefed my team, and within three months I'd doubled my email list and organised a launch that was to be my biggest yet.

I had to move forward, and if you want to change your financial future, you must too.

6. Be generous

Making generosity a practice sends a powerful message to the Universe: that we have more than enough of what we need. However, more importantly, it sends a powerful message to ourselves – and it's impossible to be stuck in a scarcity complex when you're thinking and acting generously.

As I was getting intentional about an abundant money mindset, I did a 30-day abundance challenge with meditation teacher Sah D'Simone, in which he dived deep into the concept of a scarcity complex.

Now, I had always thought this was the belief in not having 'enough', but as I discovered over those 30 days, this kind of mindset shows up in many different ways – greed and hoarding being just two examples of it.

Prior to my money story getting a good battering, I would have said I was a very generous person. But when my financial worth shrank, my propensity to be generous shrank, too.

Going through the meditation challenge really shone a light on my meanness, and how that was actively perpetuating this scarcity in my life. I genuinely didn't have a lot of cash to splash, however I did take some action – for example, I set up a monthly contribution to Kiva, which gives micro-loans to people all over the world, and built a give-back element into a monthly event series I ran, which generated thousands of dollars for charity. I also doubled down on buying and sending thank-you cards.

These actions were transformational. Firstly, because I got so much joy from being able to send cash to those who needed it and put smiles on the faces of those who received my thank-you cards. And secondly, because these small acts of abundance made me *feel* abundant, and ushered a whole new energy into my approach to money.

I must be clear here: generosity doesn't need to be limited to giving money. It may be that – right now – you don't have it to give. However, we can be generous in other ways. Sending a thank you card costs the same as a cafe cappuccino. As you gain momentum with low-cost acts of generosity and money starts to flow into your life, then you can extend your generosity to financial contributions. Just, please, don't wait until the cash rolls in to start.

7. Practise affirmations

I've talked a lot about affirmations over the years in my work, and we talked about them back in Chapter 10. For me they are very, very powerful. In my experience they train my brain to believe that what I want is already in existence.

If creating more financial success in your life is currently sitting on your To Do list, then I strongly recommend you incorporate some abundance-focused affirmations into your affirmation practice. (And if you haven't started a practice yet, what are you waiting for?!)

In your bonus Step Into You playbook I've included my favourite abundance affirmations as part of the 201 affirmations to be found there.

Denise Duffield-Thomas shared her most effective ones with me when I interviewed her for my podcast. They are:

'It's my time and I'm ready for the next step.'
'I serve, so I deserve.'
Said in the mirror:
'This is what a wealthy woman looks like.'

8. Visualise the abundant life you want to have

Where we're at financially is sometimes a *long* way from where we want to be. For example, when I was facing the horrible reality of being $30,000 in debt on my credit card, I felt like an absolute, utter dickhead for allowing that to happen. The debt was crippling to my energy, my motivation and my very soul. The idea of not having that burden was almost unimaginable.

Almost, but not quite.

If I got really, really brave I was able to manage a weak mental picture of one day logging into my credit card online and seeing the balance at zero. So I visualised that day – a lot. Over time the vision became stronger and easier for me to see. I started chipping away at the debt, and with each bank transfer over to my credit card, that zero-balance day inched closer.

Finally, after months of visualising/transferring, visualising/transferring, Zero Balance Day arrived. (Funnily enough, I paid the last couple of thousand dollars off just before I recorded a podcast episode on the very topic of this chapter!)

Since that day 12 months ago, I have paid off the credit card in full every month, and haven't paid a dollar of interest.

Choose an event that represents the fruits of you building your abundant money mindset – it might be holding the keys to your first home, seeing a certain figure in your savings account, hitting a target in your business, or being able to treat someone you love to a special surprise. Choose the event that most resonates with you, and visualise it daily.

It's possible our brains cannot tell the difference between an event happening in reality and happening in our minds. So get visualising and get ready to see your dreams become a living, breathing reality.

9. Watch your self-talk

As we've already discussed, our inner monologue governs the exact reality that we create in our lives. And, just as we talked about in Chapter 9, if we don't keep an ear out for when the sentiment of that self-talk is heading south, then we can create (or maintain) rather shitty circumstances in our lives rather quickly.

You won't be surprised when I impart the news that your thoughts can influence your financial situation positively . . . or negatively.

I'll give you an example from my life. At the end of every month, my team of contractors invoices me for the work they've done for my business over the previous month. When I was stuck in a yucky scarcity mindset, I'd see the invoices landing in my inbox, one after the other, and I'd start to panic. Then, when the time came to do the actual paying, I'd panic again. I'd log into my online bank account and pay each supplier invoice, each time seeing the balance of my account go down. My self-talk ran something like this: *'Crap, the account is getting low . . . What if there isn't enough cash to pay everyone this month? How does money go out as quickly as it comes in? Am I ever going to get ahead?'* You get the idea. The whole exercise was painful and I dreaded the end of each month for that exact reason.

Then, one day, I caught myself in the act of this horrible self-talk and gave myself a mental slap on the wrist. I remembered a great tip that entrepreneur and author Marie Forleo shared in an email newsletter, and I started practising it. Every time I paid an invoice, I said to myself (often aloud!): *'There's plenty more where that came from.'* I said it over and over and over again, until all the invoices were paid.

It didn't happen overnight, but in time there *was* plenty more – and given that Marie's business is a stonkingly successful multi-million dollar enterprise, and that her own personal net worth is estimated at US$14 million, I trust her!

I also like to remember the late Louise Hay's perspective on bills. She said that she was always grateful when a bill arrived, as it meant that some person or organisation trusted her enough to give her goods or services on credit. Louise's viewpoint has changed the whole energy I feel when I see everything from rent and mortgage to insurances and phone bills go out of our bank accounts.

10. Celebrate the money wins of others

It's very easy, when we're feeling the lack of something in our lives, to feel envious or even angry towards others who appear to have that elusive thing we're seeking.

After we experienced our two miscarriages, Wade and I took a one-year break from trying to bring babies into the world. And I swear that in that year the entire world got pregnant! Best friends, my sister, celebrities, women in my community who had told me they'd lost babies at the same time we had . . . there were a *lot* of pregnancy and birth announcements. It stung like hell.

I had similar experiences with money during those couple of years of financial stress. It's hard to be happy for someone's new house, record business revenue years or designer clothes when you're doing the 3 am money-worry wake-ups. However, I realised that being grudging of others' financial wins was directly blocking my own success in that area. It was scarcity complex dressed up in the clothes of jealousy.

So I started being happy for other people's successes. It didn't come easily. I approached it like a meditation practice: each time I felt the burn of financial envy, I'd notice that feeling, accept it, and then actively change my thoughts towards joy and celebration for that person.

A few months into this practice, a friend shared that her latest program launch had generated $120,000 in revenue – and I was *so happy* for her. It was a real measure for me of how far I'd come. (I must also note that this particular friend is one of those magical people who experiences others' wins like they're hers – and I have no doubt that that supports her financial wins no end.)

Celebrating rather than envying the success of others is an infinitely more constructive approach, not least because when someone else has a win they become a model for what's possible for us.

11. Ask for it!

Our next step in building an abundant money mindset is to actually *ask* for what it is we want. Once we get clear on what our goal is, the Universe has an uncanny way of stepping in and making that goal a reality.

In my first business, I would encourage my team to share their personal goals so that we could support each other in achieving them. At the beginning of a fresh new year, Eddy on my team said that his travel goal was 'a cheap holiday to Bali'. My point to him was that if you ask for a cheap holiday, you'll get a cheap holiday. I suggested he set a goal of a luxury holiday; then, if he fell somewhere between luxe and cheap, he'd be doing well!

In her chat with my Mastermind group, Barb de Corti spoke of how her parents had owned a business that was owed a lot of money by its customers, and that Barb's own family felt the pinch as a result. Barb got so fed up with this situation that she adopted the role of debt collector, going from door to door asking for the many outstanding bills to be paid to her parents. She was nine years old.

As I pointed out to Barb when she related this story, she learnt early on that if you want money, you need to ask for it. Can you imagine how much that early lesson served her in building her multi-million dollar revenue?!

Deciding *what exactly we want* is a critical step in manifesting our money dreams. I've noticed that the clearer I am on my money goals, the more likely I am to achieve them. And the great thing about money is that it's easy to measure! It's difficult to know if you're 20 per cent happier year on year, but you sure as hell can tell if you've got 20 per cent more savings than you did 12 months ago.

Get crystal clear on what your money goal is, ask for it and fling everything you've got at making it a reality.

12. Upgrade your life

The concept of life upgrades was something I learnt from Denise Duffield-Thomas, and it has been instrumental in getting my money mindset back on track. Denise teaches that we can divide everything in our lives into four distinct camps, in line with the tiers of airline classes: so, Economy, Premium Economy, Business and First Class.

Denise believes that when we have too much Economy Class in our lives (that is, possessions that are underperforming, broken, don't fit or stained) it pulls our money mindset down: we feel like we don't have much money and we perpetuate that cycle by living our lives that way.

At the same time, when we recognise the First Class elements in our lives (things we would still have even if we had all the money in the world) we luxuriate in that feeling of abundance.

The idea is that we identify where 'upgrades' are needed, and over time start to improve our lives.

I was shocked at how much Economy Class I had been putting up with in my life when I started out on my money mindset over-haul. And the funny thing was that it wasn't the 'big ticket' items like tech, our house and my clothes: it was the small things that I used sometimes multiple times a day that pulled me down the most.

The perfect example was our blender. We had a cheap smoothie maker that we used every single day. It was way beyond its finest days – the plastic beakers it came with were scratched, smoothie liquid had got into the base of it, making it smelly, and – worst of all – in its final days some ants had moved into it. Gross!

As soon as I identified it was Economy Class I went out and bought a gorgeous new glass blender. It wasn't a top-of-the-range one, however it was a huge leap up from what we had been using. A year later and I still get a little upgrade buzz when I make our smoothies.

Since the blender upgrade I've been slowly completing upgrades in my life, including:

- finally replacing the phone holder in the car with one that doesn't fall down every ten minutes (cost: $45)
- getting a second phone charger for my office (cost: $20)
- having five year's worth of dings, dents and cracked light covers on our lovely car fixed up (cost: $1,000)
- replacing my four-year-old wallet that Lexi had doodled all over with a shiny new one (cost: $100)
- changing our mismatched and chipped dinnerware over to a beautiful terracotta set that makes every meal feel like a restaurant meal (cost: $80)

I used to think that abundance was a destination – e.g. 'I'll feel abundant when I have $10,000 saved', or 'I'll feel abundant when I can buy whatever I want at my favourite store'. However, what I've learnt is that abundance is a *feeling*. And when we can construct our lives in such a way that we're feeling that abundance every day, we're aligning ourselves with the energetic frequency of abundance . . . and we then generate even more of it in our lives.

13. Pass it on

Now, the last thing I want to share is to pass it on. If you find something that helps you in this chapter – and I hope you do! – please share it with another woman: maybe a team member, your sister, your daughter, a friend.

As I mentioned at the outset of this chapter, we women have a long way to go to making money a topic that we can talk about openly and positively. I'm still not 100 per cent confident sharing what I have in this chapter. I'm uncertain as to what people will make of what I've written: Maybe they'll think that I'm showing off how much money I've made, or that I'm not making as much as I 'should' be? Money is fertile ground for self-doubt and self-censorship!

My hope is that this chapter sparks a conversation for you with other women.

Please remember: ~~~~~~~~

- Financially empowered women can change the world.
- Money can be an especially sensitive topic for women to discuss as we don't talk about it as much as men do, and having financial influence is relatively new for us.
- Every setback can be a comeback.
- Our money stories are behind every belief and experience we have with money.
- A regular gratitude practice will interrupt negative thought patterns about money.
- Generosity is the ideal counterbalance to a scarcity complex.

- Being genuinely happy for others and their money wins will help us on our way to our own wins.
- Abundance is a feeling, not a destination.

Chapter 15

STEPPING INTO
YOUR SEXUALITY

WE'RE ALMOST AT THE END OF OUR JOURNEY TOGETHER, AND now is the perfect time to address what I've found myself – and noticed in other women – to be a supremely challenging hotspot. That hotspot is sex.

A year ago now, I hit record on what was the most toe-curlingly revealing podcast episode I've ever created. Part of a broader season on the Step Into You theme, I shared the story of how I had reclaimed my sexuality.

I flip-flopped several times on whether or not I should put that story out there. What finally tipped me over to 'yes, share it' was the fact that this particular topic had been a source of enormous pain and shame for me . . . for years. I figured that I couldn't possibly be the only woman suffering over the same issue, so surely, if I shared my story, it could potentially help a handful of other women?

It turns out there were a *lot* more than a handful of women who were helped! The episode was downloaded thousands of times – three times more than a standard episode – and I received hundreds of DMs, emails and texts from women in every area of my life and community. The overriding sentiment was: 'Thank you so much for talking about this! I thought it was just me, and I feel so much better now.'

After the response to the episode, I knew that a chapter on sex needed to be in this book. Sex is one of the most fundamental, motivating and pleasurable elements of being human – especially, I would say, as a woman (though I'm clearly biased on that – ha!). Having journeyed into my own interest in sex, and reclaimed it, I can tell you that life is infinitely more exciting and empowering on that journey.

While I'm excited to share this with you, I do have two 'disclaimers' I'd like to make.

First off, I would consider myself an authority on a few select topics: entrepreneurship, organisation, mindset, energy management, maybe even spirituality, but I am absolutely *not* an expert on sex. My approach to this chapter is very much one of a woman who has been on a certain journey and wants to pass on to other women the insights she gained on that journey.

As this is such an incredibly personal topic, I'm not approaching this chapter with checklists, how-to guides and worksheets. Instead, I'm sharing my story in the hope that you glean some nuggets that you can apply in your own life.

Secondly, I fully acknowledge that the topic of sex can be a difficult one for some of us. At best, it might be anxiety-inducing. At worst, it might trigger past trauma. My intent with this chapter is to create a safe space to discuss this topic, and I hope it feels that way to you.

THE BACKSTORY

At the time this particular chapter of my life began to unfold, Wade and I had been together for 11 years. And, for at least the last four of those years, sex had been a significant stressor in our relationship.

A relationship counsellor we saw years ago listed the five 'horsemen' of relationship issues. They were:

1. money
2. sex
3. in-laws
4. housework
5. parenting

Well, Wade and I had had our fair share of strife with all of these issues, except the last one! However, sex was – we both now agree – the biggest issue. The problem, plain and simple, was this: Wade wanted sex a lot more than I did. In fact, I hardly wanted sex at all. (Now that I've done my research into this, I know that the technical description is 'a mismatch of libido'.)

And I took 100 per cent of the blame – actually, 200 per cent of the blame – for this issue in our relationship.

I cannot adequately convey how much stress, shame and self-hatred I directed towards myself for this state of affairs, and it became a pressure cooker in our relationship.

Wade – understandably – wanted us to talk and find a way of figuring it out. However, my own sense of shame and inadequacy held me back, as did my substandard communication skills when it came to tackling such a highly charged topic.

What intensified this shame spiral was the fact that, after Wade and I 'got serious', I never spoke to my friends about sex. I remember, back in our days of singledom, how sex was a super-fun topic amongst us. Our sex-related conversations were sometimes outrageous, sometimes mortifying, but always bonding. Then, as we coupled up and found our long-term life partners, things changed. Sex was no longer on the conversation agenda. Maybe that was because there weren't as many exciting 'developments' to report as in the early days of a relationship. There might also have been an element of protection in action. Discussing the most intimate details of a romantic relationship might have felt like we were betraying our partner's confidence. And when kids came on the scene, there was a lot more at stake for our relationships.

Whatever the reason, I wasn't talking to my close girlfriends about sex. I had zippo idea what they were up to, how their libidos were travelling, whether they and their partners were having similar conversations to Wade and me . . . It was like there was a cone of silence surrounding the entire topic. They didn't bring it up, I didn't bring it up, and I felt I was operating in a vacuum.

Research professor Brené Brown identifies these three essential ingredients to shame: judgement, secrecy and silence. Well, I was doing a stellar job of judging myself (harshly), and the lack of sharing with other humans ticked both the secrecy and the silence boxes.

It had got to the point that Wade and I couldn't talk about sex at all. As soon as he raised the topic, I would have a physiological reaction and shut down completely.

The result? I was convinced that there was something wrong with me. I had some serious fixing of myself to do.

TRYING TO 'FIX' MYSELF

I went to Bali for a week of solo retreat time, and before I left I booked a de-armouring treatment with a healer there. If you haven't heard of de-armouring before, I'll give you the nutshell version. The idea is that women store a lot of stress and trauma in their reproductive system – and that tension builds up over time. Through a series of techniques (essentially, intimate massage), that tension can be released and processed, and the tissues can heal. The benefits are also felt on an emotional level. I had sensed that I was harbouring some trauma in my system. I identified three likely causes: some procedures to treat pre-cancerous cells on my cervix in my early twenties, the episiotomy that had been required at Lexi's birth, and my two pregnancy losses.

I had three treatments while I was in Bali, and experienced huge releases from each. I expected to go back to Australia with a raging sex drive, however my expectations were somewhat unrealistic! I'm so glad I did the treatments, however, as they were very cleansing energetically, and I also can see, looking back, that they heralded the beginning of a longer healing and expanding journey.

At home, we headed into the uncertainty of the global pandemic, and Wade and I also headed into the fire with our relationship. Being at home together 24/7 brought to light how much work we needed to do on our relationship, and with the help of a magician of a relationship therapist, Dr Robert Maciver, we rolled up our metaphorical sleeves and got started.

Something Robert identified early on in our time with him was the fact that Wade and I rarely made eye contact. I had noticed this, too. Heartbreakingly, there were probably entire days that slipped past without me looking Wade square in the eyes and really *seeing him* – as my lover and romantic chosen one, rather than as a co-parent, joint household CEO and business sounding board.

Robert explained that without eye contact it was impossible to feel connected. He explained: 'Unless you're both connected, it is impossible to heal anything in your relationship.'

So our 'homework' was to get connected – to make the effort to look each other in the eye, have multiple hugs a day, and so on. Over time our connection was being rebuilt, and I began to feel brave enough to have the sex conversation with Wade, but only with Robert's facilitation. The conversation was incredibly healing and it felt like a bridge had been built between us to talk about sex together.

While Wade and I were in the midst of this work together, I began to experience physical symptoms of the stress I was feeling, chiefly in the form of intense night sweats. After investigations from my GP showed no physiological issues, I sought the help of an acupuncturist. Maggie immediately got a handle on what was going on with my body. She explained that women are in their 'yin' or feminine energy at night-time, and my stress was causing an imbalance in my yin energy.

An unexpected benefit of the sessions was that I started to feel an uptick in my libido. When I asked her about this, Maggie wasn't at all surprised, as increased sexual desire goes hand in hand with a woman being more balanced in her feminine energy.

THREE FACTS THAT CHANGED THE GAME FOR ME

Now that things were feeling immeasurably better – physically from the acupuncture, and emotionally from the revived connection with Wade – I felt brave and curious enough to start exploring the topic of sex. I researched online, read books and listened to podcasts – and I want to share with you my three biggest a-ha! moments.

1. We need to rethink the concept of 'normal'

I read about a women's studies lecturer at an Ivy League university in the US who, in 2020, was the first to teach a specific class on sex: the context of sex in society, societal norms and expectations around sex. At the end of semester she set her class an exam, and in it she posed the question, 'What has been your biggest learning from this class?' She got hundreds of completed exams back to mark, and the response to her open-ended question was almost unanimous: 'I learned that I'm normal.'

Wow!

The lecturer had had no idea that women carried such a weight of expectation relating to sex, and that almost all of them had assumed that there was something fundamentally 'wrong' with them. To have sex discussed in an open and educational setting had made them realise that there is no 'normal' when it came to sex – that everyone's individual experience is as valid, and acceptable, as the next person's.

This was huge for me, too. Surely, if that university group of women were normal, maybe, just maybe, I was 'normal' too?

2. Our sexuality is sovereign

This was a self-realisation after much reading and thinking in the early days of my exploration: at some point, my sexuality had blended into Wade's. After 11 years together, it wasn't clear where mine ended and his began, and vice versa. But bigger than that, I realised that I had always defined my sexuality with the person I was in a sexual relationship with. Sex was something that happened with them, and not something I saw as my own autonomous space.

I had come to see my sexual identity as fitting around Wade's needs, rather than being something for me to have primary ownership and enjoyment of. This was a tricky place to be, as given that Wade was unhappy with the sex we were having, in my mind that was a direct attack on my very identity.

I had carried so much guilt for falling short in this space. However, what I started to wrap my head around was that my sexuality was a sovereign nation of its own, and that by holding myself back from enjoying sex, it wasn't Wade I was falling short for, it was myself.

3. Boredom is a huge factor

A third insight came via an episode of my friend Kylie Camps's podcast, *The Frae*. In it, she interviewed sex expert Dr Wednesday Martin. What Wednesday shared turned my perspective on my situation on its head.

She said that the experience of having a 'low libido' was extremely common amongst women. She also identified that, in our society, we expect men to have higher expectations when it comes to sex; that it's men who are motivated to seek out sexual excitement. Dr Wednesday then said that men experience a drop in sexual desire approximately ten years into a monogamous relationship.

This next fact blew my mind . . . Women experience that drop in sexual desire *just one to four years* into a monogamous relationship. Dr Wednesday said that she constantly had women come to her saying they just didn't feel like sex anymore. But when she asked them if they'd like to have sex with someone other than their partner, they said that yes, they'd absolutely be excited about that!

The same week these revelatory moments were rolling in, Wade and I were on our way to the cinema for an afternoon date, and he in some way referenced sex in our conversation. Now, normally this would be my cue for instant shutdown. However, very conversationally I said, 'That's an area I've been thinking about a lot.' He was so used to me clamming up that this 'relaxed Lorraine' was a total anomaly. After the movie we went for dinner at a local pub, and he asked me to fill him in. So I did. The summary of what I shared would be this: 'Babe, I've realised: I'm just bored! So fucking bored! And it's nothing to do with you. I mean, look at you – you're the best, the hottest, so sexy . . . but I'm bored. I feel like our sex life is predictable and I'm not excited about it.'

My husband is an amazingly tolerant person, as he took this all in very calmly. He told me later that he was torn between being apprehensive as to where these revelations might take me, and ecstatic that I was actually talking to him about sex!

REWIRING MY BRAIN

Despite these powerful realisations, I was still certain I needed to do some serious work on myself, and so I decided to explore Rapid Transformation Therapy (RTT), a form of hypnosis.

RTT practitioner Rachel Crethar assured me she could help, and so we booked in our first session. During our work, I explained to her that I wanted to clear any subconscious limitations that were holding me back from experiencing my sexuality in a more open and uninhibited way.

While I was in a hypnotic state, Rachel helped me identify three life experiences that were potentially limiting me, and we worked through them together. She then guided me through a hypnotic healing, and told me to listen to that healing every day for 30 days – which I did.

THE MAKE LORRAINE SEXY AGAIN PLAN

While the RTT was working its magic, I decided that the Lorraine Sex Factor needed a boost, if not a total overhaul! What with working mostly from home and having a limited social calendar, Wade was used to seeing me at my fugliest around the house (read: baggy tracksuit bottoms and comfy underwear), and I can't say that I felt especially sexy. I wanted to change that.

So I wrote myself an action plan, and called it the 'Make Lorraine Sexy Again Plan'. (This is exquisitely mortifying to share with you. However, in the interests of the common sex-good, I am putting it down here in black and white!)

The basis of this plan came from the question: 'If I was back on the dating scene, what would I be doing differently?' I need to be clear: I had no intentions of actually *going* back on the dating scene, but I wanted to mentally explore what I would look and feel like if I was a sex entity all to myself.

I came up with four responses:

1. *I would be groomed* – feel and look the best I could.
2. *I would look amazing naked* – have a fit, toned body and glowing skin.
3. *I would dress to feel and look brilliant* – wear gorgeous underwear, stop saving my favourite clothes, and wear heels where possible (#mumlife, #wfhlife).
4. *I would be playful with sex* – create exciting experiences with sex.

Those four responses became the basis of my Make Lorraine Sexy Again Plan. In detail, this entailed the following:

• I washed my tanning mitt. This is the perfect example of how a small block prevents us from doing something that would make us feel great! I hadn't self-tanned in an eternity, as my mitt desperately needed to be washed. I got it fresh again, and tanning recommenced.

- I got eyelash extensions . . . and went a bit too hard on the sex factor. I opted for the 'Russian volume' option and ended up looking like a rookie drag queen!

- I changed my exercise routine. I'd got somewhat relaxed about my exercise regimen, so I joined a new Pilates studio and committed to doing five classes per week. Soon I felt fit, toned and stronger than I had in years.

- I overhauled my underwear drawer. My bras and knickers sat at either end of a spectrum: one end was 'comfortable, bordering on daggy', the other was 'date night' sets. The latter were pretty uncomfortable and therefore could only be worn for a handful of hours at a time. An overhaul was conducted: out went anything ill-fitting or outright tired, and I had a mini spree in an under-wear store – the first time I had ever done that. The result was six new sets of perfectly fitting underwear, beautiful enough to make me feel fabulous but comfortable enough for me to wear every day.

- I cleared my wardrobe. I gave away anything that felt heavy or didn't feel in line with the lighter/brighter/sexier me I was channelling.

- I invested in some toys. We had dabbled in sex toys over the years, however anything we had at this point had been chosen by Wade, and while I enjoyed them, they weren't setting me on fire. Part of getting more playful about sex was me exploring toys that *I* wanted. For my birthday I asked Wade for a toy, and together we went to Honey Birdette – a brand created by women for women. There I got the full lowdown from the sales assistant, which in itself was a mark of how far I'd come. To be talking about the intricacies of vibrators would have had me blushing a couple of months earlier! I made my selection and, later on that night, I wondered where this new BFF had been all my life.

THE CHANGE I EXPERIENCED

I can tell you, along with the work with Rachel, this plan changed my life. It was like I came alive sexually again. I began to explore sex solo, and dive deeper sexually with Wade.

It changed my relationship with myself. For the first time in my life, it felt like I was in the driving seat of my own sexuality, and I got to make sex as fun and exciting as I wanted. I re-engaged with the possibilities of sex again. I experienced my body in new ways. Up until my work with Rachel, I had only ever experienced clitoral orgasms. It blew my mind when I had my first G-spot orgasm . . . at the age of 38. It was like a door had opened in my mind – and on the other side of that door was possibility, and excitement.

It also changed my relationship with Wade. Now, I am not for a moment putting our relationship out there as a model for the 'right' way to do this sex thing. Like every area of a relationship, it ebbs and flows, and what works for us may not work for others. But I found that, first of all, we actually spoke about sex. It wasn't always easy, but it wasn't the walled-up space that it had been in previous years. And as I mentioned in Chapter 4, it helped me access my feminine energy and helped him tune into his masculine energy. This established more of a polarity in our relationship, just like two magnets – the same poles will repel each other but what attracts the magnets together is the connection of opposites! It also massively reduced the bickering between us. As I've mentioned before, when we have that intimate connection, it's as if a herd of unicorns sprinkling glitter and rainbows has descended on our household. All feels right in the world, and we are infinitely more loving to each other. It's the ultimate reset.

I couldn't tell you exactly which element of my campaign to step back into my sexuality was the critical one, but I believe it was a combination of the RTT rewiring my brain and also stepping into my power and reclaiming that special part of my life again, for me.

AN INVITATION TO YOU

Step one to stepping into our sexuality is to normalise talking about it, and I hope that this chapter will start a very important conversation for you. I've talked to so many women about my experience, now – friends, mentees and women in my community. And I can tell you they are *dying* to talk about sex. So if this chapter has sparked your interest, I encourage you to start talking to your friends about sex. I bet you'll find they're as keen as you to open up about it!

Please remember:

- If sex is a challenge in your relationship, consider focusing on getting connected with each other in other ways as a first step in coming together.
- You may find acupuncture supports your body in finding more hormonal balance, and potentially boosting your libido.
- There is no normal when it comes to sex.
- Our sexual identity is ours alone, even though it can feel like it's irrevocably enmeshed with our partner's.
- It's likely that women need more variety than men in the bedroom.
- Consider designing your own Make You Sexy Again Plan to help you re-engage with sex.
- Explore talking to girlfriends about sex – you may be pleasantly surprised at where the conversations go.

Conclusion

WE NEED YOUR POWER

THIS IS IT MY DEAR, THE END OF OUR STEP INTO YOU JOURNEY together (for now!). You and I have covered a lot of ground in these pages.

First, we blasted some common negative beliefs out of the water with potent truth bombs. Then we cleared the way for you to upgrade your life by easing the overwhelm that so many women feel burdened with day to day. Next, we dived deep into the idea of energy management and I shared the inside track on how you can live your life from the interest in your energy account, rather than from your capital. We discussed the difference between feminine and masculine energy, and explored strategies to help you access that nourishing feminine energy. I debunked the concept of self-care, and instead invited you to treat yourself like a top-of-the-range car . . . which means keeping your tank filled up regularly!

We then (hopefully) relieved the pressure you may have been feeling about your purpose for being in this world, and you guided yourself through some Big Questions to help define your purpose, passion and vision. From there, we kicked into motivation mode – helping you get ready to do some powerful thinking about where you want your life to be, including articulating your Dream Lifestyle. And *then* we got into the nuts and bolts of goal setting, when I stepped you through my goal-setting process.

With your goals tucked into your metaphorical handbag, it was time to set you up for max success by making them a reality. I shared the concept of resistance, and how we can learn to dance with it. That said, our own self-sabotaging patterns can happen, making it grindingly difficult to deliver the goods with our goals. So, we talked through the five biggest pitfalls to staying on track – and what you can do about them. We forsook the ever-elusive idea of balance, and instead committed to seeking alignment in our lives – including how to know when we're falling out of alignment. As you now know, every top performer needs their support team around them – and I introduced eight types of experts who can guide you towards the best version of you.

Then it was time for the hotspots. First up, we tackled the potential minefield that is setting and maintaining boundaries. Then I shared – in painful detail sometimes – the story of my own journey towards an abundance mindset, and how you can leverage the tools I used (and continue to use). And the sharing continued as I guided you through my experience of stepping into my sexuality.

Wow, we *did* cover a lot, didn't we?!

But we're not done just yet. I've got two crucial points to share with you before you head off into your dream future.

YOU DON'T NEED PERMISSION

I've seen in my work with women through mentoring, retreats, events and programs that so often they are waiting for permission to strike out and make the changes they wish to make in their lives.

I've experienced this phenomenon myself – feeling that it's selfish, self-indulgent or weak to prioritise my needs and desires, whether that's going on a retreat, taking a day off or changing my mind about a commitment. I've wrestled with the side of me that knows what's best for me, and the side that wants to people-please or not upset the status quo. And it's exhausting! I've (often) asked Wade for permission to do something – to which he responds with absolute confusion as to why I'm even considering that I need his say-so.

As we covered earlier in the book, women are raised to prioritise the needs of others over their own, epitomising the patriarchal ideal of the selfless female. In a conversation with my friend and fellow author/entrepreneur Alexx Stuart, she posed this powerful question: 'Who benefits from you being tired?' Think about it: if women are too exhausted, overwhelmed or cowed to challenge the way things have 'always been done', then nothing changes.

And we need change; we need it now. For ourselves first and foremost, but also for the vibrant and potential-filled generation of women coming up after us. And the generation after that and the generation after that.

That change starts with us stepping into our full potential and power. And you need no-one's – no-one's! – permission to do that. Give *yourself* permission *right now*, and feel the empowerment and inspiration that comes with it.

As one of my lady-heroes Glennon Doyle wrote in her book *Untamed*: 'This life is mine alone. So I have stopped asking people for directions to places they've never been.'

YOU'RE CAPABLE OF MORE THAN YOU COULD EVER IMAGINE

I want you to know that you are wonderful. You are brave, you are strong and you are endlessly resourceful. Life can be tough, people can be mean and we can be knocked down over and over again. But look at you! You're here! And you're *still* seeking and learning.

I've experienced pain and challenge – less than some, more than others – but if there's one thing I know for sure, it's that on the other side of that pain and challenge is a stronger, brighter, more beautiful me. And you are the very same.

You might remember that my intent at the outset of this book was to create an infrastructure that would help you step into the lightest and brightest version of you possible. I truly hope you feel you've got that infrastructure right here in your hands and can use it to take yourself to new heights, because we all have potential beyond our wildest dreams. Author Sue Monk Kidd once wrote that we should do at least one thing in our lives that takes our own breath away.

FROM HERE

I hope I've started a ripple effect that you will carry on long after you put this book on your bookshelf . . .

Get talking about the ideas I've shared, and the insights you've had. Change starts with us, but it continues by us having conversations about the changes we're experiencing. Never underestimate the power of a conversation to have a profound impact on someone else's life.

Join the conversation by connecting with me on Instagram, @lorraineremarks. I love love *love* hearing from my readers! Tell me what your biggest takeout was from this book and one action you're committing to.

Listen to my podcast, *The Lorraine Murphy Show*, for lots more ideas, experts and tried and tested tips that I'm currently applying in my life, and read some of the inspiring books from my curated reading list that follows.

Make your Step Into You Playbook your BFF. Prioritise *you* by working through the exercises, and feel free to revisit it and redo the exercises for years to come.

Most of all, remember this: take your own breath away.

READING LIST

I INVITE YOU TO CONTINUE YOUR JOURNEY INTO THE MOST HIGH-RES version of yourself with these books. I've gleaned useful nuggets and new perspectives from them, and some have been downright life-changing.

Becoming Supernatural: How common people are doing the uncommon

Joe Dispenza

Read it for: how we can upgrade our energy to align with more possibility and potential in our lives.

Beyond Mars and Venus: Relationship skills for today's complex world

John Gray

Read it for: a guide to navigating modern relationships, and a deep dive into the world of masculine and feminine energy.

Braving the Wilderness: The quest for true belonging and the courage to stand alone

Brené Brown

Read it for: an understanding of what belonging means in today's world, and how we can brave discovering our own truth.

Comparisonitis: How to stop comparing yourself to others and be genuinely happy

Melissa Ambrosini

Read it for: a solution-oriented approach to minimising the impact of 'comparisonitis' on your happiness.

Daily Rituals: Women at work

Mason Currey

Read it for: fascinating insights into the working days of creative women spanning three centuries.

Dear Lover: A woman's guide to men, sex, and love's deepest bliss

David Deida

Read it for: an insight into what women *really* want from their men.

Do the Work: Overcome resistance and get out of your own way

Steven Pressfield

Read it for: a deep dive into resistance, and how we can tackle it to prevent it from stifling our creativity and productivity.

Fair Play: A game-changing solution for when you have too much to do (and more life to live)

Eve Rodsky

Read it for: a briefing on the impact of the mental load, and a genius approach to democratising the 'thinking' with our partners.

Fed Up: Emotional labor, women, and the way forward

Gemma Hartley

Read it for: an understanding of the concept of 'emotional labour' and what we can do about it.

Get Remarkably Organised

Lorraine Murphy

Read it for: my tried and tested approach to GSD (Getting Shit Done) – this is me in my organisational happy place! *Get Remarkably Organised* is also available as an audiobook.

Getting the Love You Want: A guide for couples

Harville Hendrix and Helen LaKelly Hunt

Read it for: an understanding of how our romantic relationships have the ability to heal us.

Girl, Wash Your Face: Stop believing the lies about who you are so you can become who you were meant to be

Rachel Hollis

Read it for: a motivating account of Rachel's own life, and her greatest life lessons.

Heal Your Body: The mental causes for physical illness and the metaphysical way to overcome them
Louise Hay
Read it for: a detailed breakdown of the physical symptoms we experience, and what the underlying mental/emotional causes are. (A mini version of this book is included at the end of *You Can Heal Your Life*.)

Loving What Is: Four questions that can change your life
Byron Katie
Read it for: a breakdown of Katie's legendary approach to 'doing The Work'. I find her exercises to be very helpful in dealing with a painful issue with a person or situation.

Open Wide: A radically real guide to deep love, rocking relationships and soulful sex
Melissa Ambrosini
Read it for: a far-reaching overview to relationships, energy and mindset.

The Midnight Library
Matt Haig
Read it for: a paradigm-shifting philosophical perspective on regrets in our lives. This is the only fiction book on this list – that's how powerful I found this novel to be!

The Way of the Superior Man: A spiritual guide to mastering the challenges of women, work, and sexual desire
David Deida

Read it for: a manual to modern day masculinity and a guide to heterosexual relationships.

Untamed: Stop pleasing, start living
Glennon Doyle
Read it for: a searing reframe on people-pleasing, and striking out in the direction of the life *we* want to live.

Untrue: Why nearly everything we believe about women and lust and infidelity is untrue
Wednesday Martin
Read it for: an investigation into lust, and Wednesday's own explorations into opening her sexual horizons.

Wintering: The power of rest and retreat in difficult times
Katherine May
Read it for: a comforting, wide-ranging read on the idea of retreating, and why it's a fundamental part of our natural cycle.

You Can Heal Your Life
Louise Hay
Read it for: an introduction to Louise's philosophy, and how affirmations hold the key to healing our past trauma, and finding wellness and happiness.

ACKNOWLEDGEMENTS

THANKS MUST GO TO THE MANY POTS OF GREEN TEA, UMPTEEN mugs of cacao and far too many squares of dark chocolate for fuelling the writing of this book. And noise-cancelling headphones, you are a legit miracle! The last stretch of the book was written and edited sitting next to Wade (aka the loudest man on Zoom ever) in our home office during an extended lockdown – a feat I never thought possible.

But seriously . . .

To you, my marvellous reader, thank you for investing in this book. I truly hope what I share in these pages serves you deeply in your life.

To the Hachette Australia team: Fiona Hazard, you immediately saw the vision for what this book could be. Thank you for believing in it, championing it, and for the cheerleading along the way. Rebecca Allen, the editing maestro! Thank you for guiding this process with such grace and skill. And Alysha Farry, Melissa Wilson, Kate Taperell and Rosina Di Marzo – the marketing and PR gurus! Thank you for helping readers find this book.

Susan Gray, thank you for treating my manuscript with care and sensitivity, and for navigating the unenviable task of keeping me on point.

Lily Partridge, you provided a beautiful inspiration for the cover of this book – you are so very talented.

Christa Moffitt, I love my cover! Thank you for making it so drop-dead gorgeous.

Sally Obermeder, you are a special light in life. Thank you for reading this manuscript while running your brilliant business, homeschooling *and* navigating a lockdown.

My LM community: to all of my mentees, podcast listeners and social media friends . . . surprise! You were the inspiration and testing ground for the ideas in this book. You are wonderful and I love that I get to have you as part of my life, and to be a part of yours.

The Make It Happen Team . . . AJ Davis, my right-hand woman/ Girl Friday/reality checker all rolled into one, thank you for the love and straight talkin' you bring to my business, and for the touch of book research moonlighting! Michelle Broadbent, I adore that our business journey continues to evolve together. Thank you for being in my corner for all these years. Bianca Deguara, you are the efficiency that keeps this whole business gig humming along. Thank you for your brilliant attention to detail and the positive energy you bring to our team.

Iva Vycichlova – biggest gratitude to you for the care and love you show our family.

Thank you to all the authors, podcasters and mentors that I have been lucky enough to learn from, and to Rachel MacDonald, Dr Robert Maciver, Claire Obeid, Ronan Powell, Jack Delosa, Denise Duffield-Thomas, Barb de Corti, Sabri Suby and Alexx Stuart for your permission to quote your work in this book.

My wonderful friends, thank you for being on this ride with me, and for the big and little ways you make life more connected and more fun . . . and for sharing WTF parenting moments.

My parents, thank you for all of the opportunities you gave to me, and for having my back in the really tough times. My darling sister, Jenny, even on the other side of the world, I can feel our closeness. Thank you for being my favourite sister. And to Blaine, Fiadh and Jamie – we miss you.

To my husband Wade, I am endlessly proud of you and the man you are. Thank you for being the ballast in a rather . . . emotional . . . household, and for the hunger for learning and growth you actively demonstrate every day in your life.

To our two shooting stars, in words inspired by Lady Gaga, I would have broken my heart to save part of you. Know that you're both safely tucked away in my heart.

To Lexi: who's clever? You! Who's kind? You! Who's brave? You! Who's funny? You! Who's loving? You! Who's so very loved? You!

And to sweet Wilder, we created this book together baby boy! Thank you for the infusion of joy and love that you've brought to our lives. How very worth the wait you were.

I'd love to hear from you!

Find out more about my work on my website (including
mentoring with me): lorrainemurphy.com.au
Connect with me on Instagram: @lorraineremarks
Listen to my podcast: *The Lorraine Murphy Show*, available
wherever you listen to your podcasts

**And explore my other books, which you can get a taste of
in the following pages . . .**

Remarkability

Remarkability is an inspiring look at the lessons Lorraine learned on her entrepreneurship journey towards becoming an award-winning businesswoman. Discover the strategies Lorraine developed and the daily habits she religiously follows to achieve her goals both in business and in life.

'If you're looking for real business insights from the trenches of a busy start-up, then look no further than this book.'

Emma Isaacs, founder of Business Chicks,
author of *Winging It* and *The New Hustle*

Get Remarkably Organised
(also available as an audiobook)

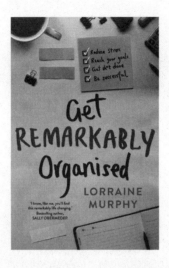

Get Remarkably Organised is Lorraine's essential guide to all things organisation. Covering everything from decluttering, planning, being proactive, developing a routine, building great habits, dealing with distractions and overcoming procrastination to blending work and home life, and staying on track – even with kids in the picture – Lorraine will show you how to master organisation and get shit done.

'I literally could not put Lorraine's book down. I began to make changes and implemented so many of her suggestions – they were easy to put into practice, with a huge, immediate payoff.'

Sally Obermeder, television presenter, radio host, author, and co-founder of SWIISH

Baby, You're Remarkable:
The no-BS guide to business with a new family

Baby, You're Remarkable is Lorraine's unfiltered, totally honest and judgement-free account of her personal (and not always perfect!) journey in running a business and having a baby. Including experiences and insights from a variety of other parents, and coupled with useful lists, suggested reading and downloads, Lorraine's story will inspire you to maintain your career while growing a family – and will show you it *is* possible to blend the two worlds.

'Lorraine's award-winning experience in business makes her the
go-to expert on how to get organised, productive and ultimately
achieve more from life. This is the book I wish I had when
I started my businesses alongside my family, but one that will
help me now achieve further growth and satisfaction.'
Angela Priestley, founding editor of Women's Agenda

Lorraine Murphy is an award-winning entrepreneur, bestselling author, speaker, mentor and mother. Lorraine founded her first business in 2012. Australia's first influencer talent agency, it grew from a start-up to multi-million dollar turnover and earned Lorraine and the business several accolades including being named as one of BRW's Fast Starters, Entrepreneur of the Year, Content Marketer of the Year, Emerging Agency of the Year and Australian Start Up of the Year. In December 2017, Lorraine sold the business to focus on her 'soul-on-fire work' – writing, speaking and mentoring. She now creates online programs, events and mentoring programs, as well as her weekly podcast, *The Lorraine Murphy Show*. Lorraine has also trained teams from brands including Uber, Unilever, Westpac and Woolworths. Lorraine lives in Sydney, Australia, is married to fellow entrepreneur Wade and is the ridiculously proud mother of their two children, Lexi and Wilder.

hachette
AUSTRALIA

If you would like to find out more about Hachette Australia,
our authors, upcoming events and new releases, you can visit
our website or our social media channels:

hachette.com.au

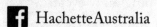 HachetteAustralia

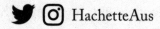 HachetteAus